# Unquiet

# Mind

A memoir by

Carol Hayes

## Prologue

The house Mama and I lived in was small—so small there was no extra room for an upright freezer. With a lack of space, we had to be creative. That's how the freezer ended up in our dining room. It was the only place it fit.

I was 18 years old back in August of 1967 and had lived through the birth of a child, a marriage, and a divorce. In that order. When Sheila was born, my mother-in-law, Grace, took her from me and Ronnie, saying she would raise her since we were too young. Grace, whom I would forever think of as The Beast, was overbearing, controlling, manipulative, and downright mean. I was a mess, my life wasn't any better, so I went back to live with Mama.

In the middle of a hot August day in Swainsboro, Georgia, I made the gruesome discovery that changed Mama's life and mine completely. Finding nothing to eat in the kitchen, I looked at the big white upright freezer in the dining room. The freezer had only one door with three metal shelves and a big pull out drawer that sat on the bottom. Opening the door it was easy to see there wasn't anything worth snacking on in there. Then my eyes drifted to the big drawer at the bottom.

At first, I thought something looked odd, out of place. "Why is there a towel in the freezer?" I reached down and slowly opened the drawer the rest of the way. With each inch of it moving towards me, I began to see what looked like a doll wrapped in a green and white striped towel. "Who put a doll in the freezer and why?" I said out loud. Was it a doll? Of course it was, but then why did I suddenly become so afraid? As the message of what I knew to be true reached my brain, panic began to brew in my body. My heart pounded in my chest and I heard it in my ears, my head spinning, about to explode. Sweat started oozing from every pore. I needed to do something. My legs needed to move. I needed to breathe, but even breath was slow to come. Finally I gasped, like someone just reaching the surface of the water. Lord, wake me up! God help me, I'm not dreaming! Where do I go?

I ran to my friend Margie's house down the street and started banging as hard as I could on the screen door, yelling all the while, "HELP, HELP!" Margie came to the door and I pleaded with her to come with me. I could see her fear even through my own. Margie was afraid, afraid of the situation, of my extreme panic, and of me. She dragged me to her neighbor's house and we pulled that neighbor along with us down the street. "Good Lord! What have you two done now?" she asked.

"It's a doll, it's a doll! Come look at the doll!" I was screaming all the way.

My heart pounded even faster now, ready to explode for sure. When we got back to my house, the door was still wide open. The screen door had been pushed so far back it remained in place like it was commanded to stay, a sentry at his post. My friend and her neighbor went into the house having no idea what they were about to encounter and had already convinced themselves I was hysterical over a doll in a freezer. Until that point in time, nothing too much happened in Swainsboro, Georgia. The biggest thrill had been when the Hell's Angels rode through town once. All that changed when I opened the freezer drawer.

 "It's not a doll" were the first words I heard after getting back into my house. "We need to call the police," followed. Who said it, I'm not sure and it didn't really matter. It could have been my friend or it could have been her neighbor. Either way, I wasn't in a bad dream, a nightmare, nor had I mistaken a doll for a baby. It was real and I was dissolving. What remained of me was an island, one that wouldn't be easily reached from that day on.

"I have to call my mama," was all I could say. What else could I do?

Chapter 1

*Grams*

Hattie Kell Gillen, my maternal grandmother, was the most precious person in my heart while growing up. Grams had taken Mama and me in when I was born and raised me from the get go. Mama was only nineteen years old when I was born and had no trouble letting Grams raise me. Mama did not have the common sense or emotional stability it took to raise a child but was kind and sweet to everyone she met.

Grams married Mr. Franklin Durham Gillen in 1924 when she was thirty-four and he was sixty-four. Mr. Frank, as she called him after the traditional southern manner of address, had been married previously to Jessie Burgess and they had ten children together at the time of her passing in 1912. Grams and Mr. Frank had only one child together, my mother. Born in 1930 she was named Jessie, perhaps after the first Mrs. Gillen which could have been a curse for Mama since it was surely never a blessing. Mr. Frank died in 1943 at the age of eighty-three and left Mama and Grams alone. Grams never remarried.

Grams was a strong, stern, no-nonsense, God-fearin', true southern woman. By the time I was born she was almost sixty and had long white hair down to her waist. She wrapped it in a bun to sit on the top of her head. It was my privilege to brush that hair every night before I went to bed and it's a memory I cherish. She had blue eyes, ivory skin, and stood about five-foot-four inches tall, but to me she was a big woman. I don't remember seeing her without glasses on her face and she read to me every day. Because of that I was reading at age three.

Grams was well known and well respected all over the little towns in and around Bishop, Georgia. She was the driving force behind the start of two churches and introduced the hot lunch program at the local school, even when the school still had a dirt floor. She wished things were different, mostly for me. She had never driven a car so we would take the Greyhound bus into Athens sometimes. It was the 1950s and the line was clear between black and white. Pulling Grams' hand every time we got on the bus I begged to sit in the back only to hear her whisper "the back is only for the coloreds." We HAD to sit in the front. Once we got to Athens, it was more of the same. Separate water fountains marked *white* or *colored*. Tables in restaurants in the back with signs on them stating *for coloreds*. I don't think any of us children understood but accepted it as just our way of life. The word colored was used back then and my apologies to anyone offended by the reference. It has to be used here.

The colored people lived at the end of town. The place they lived was like a town of its own. Wood slat houses, some barely holding on, were laid in a semi-circle. When Grams needed yard work or help in the house, we walked down to the colored area and there were always girls and boys willing to help. We went marching back to Grams with the children, we leading in front, with the little ducklings coming behind us. It had to look something like that, I reckon. Some extra girls always came and we played on my swing set but kept our distance as we had been taught. When we thought no one was watching we would sneak just a quick tag of each other and laugh, as if tempting the devil. We never talked or said a word, just smiled and laughed at each other. I think we all looked forward to those days of play.

Grams was a kind woman and went out of her way for people. I figured this out quite young. In Georgia in the sixties, prisoners were treated differently than they are today. The state had its infamous chain gangs back then. The male prisoners, both black and white, wore chains around each ankle and each chain was attached to the next prisoner. While they worked, their arms were free, but when they weren't working the shackles went back on their arms. These Georgia prisoners had to work for their keep and mostly what they did was road work; keeping the grass on the sides of the roads and railroad tracks cut down with sling blades, using that sharp hook at the end of the long handle for the job.

Since there were railroad tracks directly across the road from our house, we got to see a chain gang a few times every summer. Grams would see them first thing in the morning and it was probably the only time we locked our doors.

"Oh, Lawd, there's the chain gang! They'll be here all day. Carol, help me lock the doors and don't you go outside unless you want a switchin', now."

Grams' compassion was deep, but she was also a practical woman so I had to stay inside while the prisoners worked along the tracks. As much as she worried about me going outside while they were there, she was also concerned about their well-being in the scorching heat. One would think she was concerned mostly for the guards keeping watch over the chain gang, but that wasn't Grams' way. She worried for the worker just as much.

Grams wasn't a woman who just talked about being concerned or giving advice to others about what ought to be done, she was a woman of action, taking part in helping people when she felt it was warranted. When the chain gangs were working in the Georgia heat, it was warranted. Come noon on those days I would see Grams heading across the road with pitchers of lemonade and sweet tea for everyone. She gave them real glasses to drink from. She would give it to the guards and tell them to make sure the prisoners got some, too. I remember her saying, "It is too hot for a man to be in this heat all day with no liquid nourishment." Not intimidated by the guards one bit, Grams would tell them, "Just leave the pitchers and all by the tracks and I'll pick them up when you leave." What really struck me was the reaction of the guards and especially the prisoners. As I sat there, peeking through the drawn curtains, I saw smiles form across their faces, the gratitude obvious as they watched the old woman in the crisp, starched white apron scurry back to her house. It might have even been a little comical if they hadn't been prisoners and Grams hadn't been so serious about locking the doors.

Everything we owned was ironed and starched including every apron Grams wore, and she wore one daily. We never left the house without our clothes being crisp and starched.

Grams' home was the house she and Mr. Frank lived in and had been pieced together long before as Mr. Frank and his first wife's family grew out of the original structure. The house was white with a large porch that wrapped three quarters around. The front door would lead into a sitting room that was rather large. There were five bedrooms, a kitchen, and a room with a toilet. That's it, a toilet, no sink and certainly no bathtub. Later a bath tub would be added, but we weren't bothered. In fact, we were living high by the standard of that time and place. Most of the town still had outhouses. It was truly a luxury to be able to use the toilet in the middle of the night without having to walk outside. Our back porch was built around a well. Right smack dab in the middle of our porch stood the well where Grams would get what she called the cookin', drinkin, and bathin' water.

Living like we did was nothing to me or anyone from our town, but my Yankee cousins from Chicago weren't used to it. They were Yankees because Uncle Austin was working for a company that transferred them to Chicago, which was Yankee land to us. Eventually I had four cousins who were the only ones I ever had. When they would visit, a huge round tin wash tub would be filled with water and all four of us girls would bathe in the tub at the same time. The one boy cousin, Cid, would get a bath of his own and even the "girly" water was thrown out the back door and filled fresh for him. Finally the well became dry and we got running water from somewhere and a real bathtub put in the house. There would never be anyone in my life as strict as my grandma, but I would later come to believe that it was her way of showing me how much she cared. When I sat in her lap, always in a rockin' chair, with her arms around me I felt as safe as a hush puppy in a cookie jar. Which was pretty darned safe.

When I was three years old we were having one of our late evening summer storms. Steady heavy rain but not much else. It had been a long while since I ate baby food out of a jar, yet I still liked the custard that came in those jars and sometimes was able to have it as a treat. This particular night I had told Mama that custard was the thing I wanted. She got the umbrella, picked me up in her arms, and proceeded to carry me in the pouring rain down the road to the only little store in the small town. As we were walking, my arms were wrapped around her neck with my cheek snuggled next to hers feeling the warmth. "I love you, Carol," Mama said. It was the first and last time she would say those words for 50 years.

Chapter 2

*Miss Jessie Comes of Age*

Grams' husband, Mr. Frank, had a son from his previous marriage named Fred. He was the man Grams had fallen for before she attached to Mr. Frank. Fred was a lawyer and a busy man. He married, but his wife died young giving birth to their only child. Mr. Fred was left alone to care for this little girl, but Grams stepped in to care for her. Lillian Roxanne was her full name. Grams brought Lillian into her home and raised her as a sister to my mama. Roxie, as she was called, was competition for Mama. Grams was already short on outward affection and having two girls competing for the short supply created competition between them. It's funny how much Grams was willing and wanted to hold me in her lap, love me, and give me hugs and kisses every day. As I grew into an adult, it became apparent to me that Grams had not showed this much affection toward Mama. I've often wondered if this behavior contributed to Mama's illness because, unfortunately, it seems to be in the family gene pool.

As Mama and Roxie fought for Grams' love, their main source of affection, Mr. Frank, died. Though his passing was expected due to his advanced age, neither of them were terribly broken up about it. They planned the funeral, and when that was over, went about their business. Seemed Mama got some of her coldness from Grams. Mama and Grams were a lot alike in that way. I was different. Grams loved me like there was no tomorrow, every day. There was nothing more important in her life and I think I knew it right away. Funny how things work. Grams and Mama being so much alike except Mama never found or felt the love that Grams and I shared.

Aunt Roxie would tell me how she had to pick cotton when she was growing up, but Grams would not allow Mama to do it. It was not ladylike and she didn't want her daughter doing that if she didn't have to. Mama used to tell me she begged to pick cotton and thought it was very mean of her mother not to let her do it when all the other kids got to. The resentment my mother felt, coupled with Grams' coolness toward her, didn't signal to me at the time that trouble was on its way for my mother. But many years of therapy later, I would learn the signs were already there. Life went on for the two girls, and when they grew up each met the men of their dreams. Roxie met a man named Austin Gray and Mama married my dad, Edd Saxon.

Edd hated his name Alvin, his given name at birth and his daddy's name. To make matters worse, his middle name was Radcliffe, which he also hated. He made it very clear to anyone who knew him that he just couldn't take both of those names together. So, at sixteen, he went to the tiny post office in Farmington and told the woman at the counter that he didn't like his name and wanted to change it. She asked what he wanted it changed to and he replied "Ed." He gave her five dollars for the legal document and later noticed she had spelled his name "Edd." Even *Ed* spelled wrong was better than *Alvin Radcliff* as far as my daddy was concerned.

Edd was about six feet tall and thin with brown hair and blue eyes. He was from another small town just down the road from Bishop called Farmington. His parents were farmers raising cows and goats and he and Mama seemed attractively fit for each other. Edd would soon join the navy and leave Mama and she would continue to live with Grams.

Austin, brown hair and blue eyes as well, was also a good-looking man and was certainly a catch for Aunt Roxie, being a more educated man than Edd and having graduated from college. Austin had taken a job in Yankee-land, Chicago, and he and Roxie would move there after the wedding.

In 1948 the double wedding of the future Mr. and Mrs. Gray and Mr. and Mrs. Saxon took place at the church two houses away from Grams house. It was truly the biggest event that ever happened in Bishop, Georgia. The church was red brick all around with a pitched roof in front and four brick columns that held up the smaller entrance roof. The church was literally a product of the townspeople, started in 1912 and finished in 1919. Everything that happened in Bishop took place at that church. It was the town haven during bad summer storms, and the ditch that separated the church from the house next door was the place whole pigs were cooked from sun up to sun down on holidays. The entire town gathered at the church often, and it represented the happiest of times for everyone, funerals being the one exception, of course. All the townsfolk funerals were held at that church.

On that beautiful summer day in 1948, both brides wore lacey white long-sleeved dresses with trains that flowed down the many steps leading to the church entrance. They each had white veils that covered their faces completely, but when the veils came off, the resemblance was unmistakable. Even though they weren't sisters by blood they came from the same blood line and it showed. There was a lot o' Irish in those girls.

The church was filled with everyone who lived in Bishop, plus many visitors from the surrounding towns. The church overflowed with flowers and guests dressed to the nines. It was like a holiday, the fourth of July and Christmas all rolled into one.

The problems for Mama started almost immediately after her wedding.  Because my daddy was in the navy he was gone most of the time. This was probably a good thing since Grams despised him. The two of them, my daddy and Grams, were like oil and water, they didn't blend. At the same time they were like gasoline and fire—combustible. Simply said, the two could never mingle. I don't have a hard time talking about my daddy; I just have a hard time calling him that. Edd and Mama were always butting heads and I was a witness to that on more than one occasion. He had already left Mama by the time I was three but came to pick me up at the house and take me to my first drive-in movie. Drive-ins were the big thing in those days and sometimes used for things other than watching a movie. Many a baby was conceived in the backseat of a car at the drive-in movies. Grams didn't want me to go, to be with such a man even if he was my daddy. They argued at the front door of the house and she told him he better have me back at such and such a time or she would call the police. That was kinda funny in itself since Mr. Willard, the town sheriff, lived next door and was the only police around until you got to Athens. By calling I think she meant she would stand on the porch and yell his name and Mr. Willard, being the gentleman he was, would have come runnin'.

Edd and I went to the drive-in and we watched the stars as much as the movie screen. We stood outside the car and pretended to count them and he showed me the Big Dipper and the little one, too. I was happy and fell asleep on the way home, waking up for only a second while he and Grams went at it about something. The first memory I have after that night was going to Edd's parents' house (my fraternal grandparents) and seeing him with a woman that I thought was fat. After getting home Mama asked me who was there so I told her about the fat woman and she said "Carol, she's not fat, she's pregnant with yo daddy's baby." That didn't mean much to me then, tender young age that I was, but years later I would think differently.

Other than the fights with Grams and the drive-in movie, I could only recall two other memories of Edd when I was young. One was that he made me a red rocking chair, with the seat and back being made of thick rope. The chair was tiny like me and fit me just right. To this day I have been cursed with always having to have a rocking chair no matter where I am. It's the first thing I look for when I enter someone's home and I still look when I stay in hotels, although I have pretty much given up ever finding one there. I only use the word cursed because there were times when I was so nervous about something that I would envision Grams holding me in a rocking chair and felt it was the only thing that would calm me. Even when I became so big that my legs would almost drag the floor, I would sit in Grams' lap until she rocked me to sleep. Other than brushing her long white hair just the thought of that time in my life still brings me comfort.

Not long after our conversation about the fat lady, Mama told me that she and Edd were getting a divorce. I was about three years old, and since he wasn't around much I am not sure I really noticed the difference. One night, a meeting took place in Grams' house between Mama and Edd to finalize the provisions of the divorce. This meeting was in the kitchen, which was directly next to my bedroom with a door that was never closed, not even during their talk. The first subject was money (isn't it always?) and I heard Mama say she didn't want anything from him. Just get out of her life! The next words I heard put together were by Mama when she said "You can't have Carol" and Edd's quick reply was "I don't want her." My feelings for the man who gave me life dissolved with the tears I tried to choke back, to no avail. At that moment I hated my daddy and would never call him anything but Edd for the rest of his life. At a very tender age, I started building walls.

## Chapter 3

*A New Daddy*

The divorce went on while Mama was going to the University of Georgia and also working at a bank in Athens, close to UGA. She would take the Greyhound bus back and forth every day for the thirty-minute ride since we didn't have a car and no one knew how to drive anyway. Neither she nor Grams ever talked about Edd. It was like he was never really a part of our lives but more like a visitor who had stopped by for a while. I never saw Mama much but relied on Grams for everything. A year had gone by since the divorce. I was four years old when Grams became all and everything to me, and I felt life might have been unbearable if not for her. Her love for me was never judgmental, always forgiving and unconditional. She woke me up in the mornings with a big hug and rocked me to sleep at night, her arms tight around me and her head resting on mine. I felt her heart beat and the warmth of her breath and it was sweet, like a rose. I wouldn't feel love like that much during my life but I did come to realize how special it was. For the next three years, Grams saw to me as any mother would—nourishing me emotionally, mentally and physically. But not always in ways you might think.

"Go get me a switch off the switch bush."

The first time I was told to do this I already knew what it meant. I thought I was being smart by picking the skinniest switch I could find. Quickly I found out that the small ones were like whips and hurt much more! Grams never switched my legs more than a couple of times nor left marks, but it was often. I could be a real handful, an only child who would push an old woman to her limits, but I always lost the game. Grams meant business. The only time she raised her voice was standing on the front porch yelling "Caaaaaroooooolll" when it was time for my nap. A nap! Every day of my life, I took a nap. Right in the middle of making a frog house out of mud or popping caps on a rock, "Annie Oakley" here had to "lay down for a while." I had to leave

Roy Rogers, Dale Evans and Hopalong Cassidy when Grams called my name. My neighbors, the only kids I had to play with, were the children of Sheriff Willard. David, Doug, and Pam were their names. Pam was the oldest and sometimes left the three of us to play cowboys and Indians by ourselves. The playing was mostly in their yard unless we got the hankering to climb the great pecan tree in Grams' front yard. "Oh my Lawd! You gonna fall from there and break your neck!" I can still hear Grams' warning voice. According to her, I was always gonna break my neck, drown, burn up from the sun, have my face freeze that way, choke on chewing gum while I slept, get impetigo, catch lice, or maybe just implode one day. Grams watched over me like a mama hen. Everything I did make her uneasy and made me want to drive her crazy.

Mr. Willard's wife was Ms. Myrtice and second to Grams they were the closest people in my life. Ms. Myrtice treated me like one of her own, and Mr. Willard was the only, and best role model I could have for a daddy and I loved him like one. Being the sheriff of Bishop didn't take a whole lot. The jail was located directly across the street and was about twelve by twelve. It had one cell which Mr. Willard locked us up in at times just for fun. It was a lot like Mayberry. The income for the family came from Mr. Willard's job driving a uniform truck. Unlike today, almost all companies like restaurants and auto shops had the employees uniforms cleaned, starched and pressed for them. Mr. Willard picked up the uniforms and delivered them back to the business they came from. He got home at the same time every day. All of us would anticipate his arrival by jumping rope right outside the front door. Double Dutch. Two of us turning two ropes in the opposite direction while reciting something like "one strike, two strikes, three strikes you're out." On the word *out* the one inside the swinging ropes had to jump out while keeping the ropes swinging smoothly and another person jumped in. With four of us and each one taking a turn at jumping and swinging the ropes we could keep it going for a long time. Long enough for Mr. Willard to pull in the driveway in the uniform truck. The ropes stopped as we all ran and jumped on him as if he were a hero home from battle. Even his own children felt that much affection for both their parents. They included me in all their activities and were the only family I had for years.

After the divorce from my dad, Mama dated several men, some of them from the Bishop area, but nothing ever came of those dates. One afternoon she came home from work beaming like I had never seen her before. Mama was amiable but usually didn't show much emotion and kept to herself most of the time. She had met a man and he had asked her out. Mama was beside herself with happiness and at the age of six I was happy, too. It was hard to tell what she was thinking most of the time, during this period and throughout her life. She could usually be found sitting in the porch swing smoking cigarettes and watching shadows of the wood slats move across the bottom of her feet as the swing gently moved to and fro.

She could not stop talking about *the man*. His name was J.W. (it was the first time I had heard of someone's name bein' just letters) and that stood for John William. He was a Georgia State Trooper, six feet tall and handsome with eyes so dark they reminded you of coal. He was bald on top of his head but the slight hair he did possess blended with the color of coal in his eyes. Dark like an approaching storm but not threatening. They had met at a cafeteria and "Oh yes, he's bald" Mama warned us as if that were a strike against him. Grams' first reaction was not a good one. As I mentioned before, Grams was a stern woman and didn't particularly like men to begin with and now another one was gonna cause more trouble. She started in on Mama about how she had a daughter to raise and should be spending more of her time doing that than chasing down some man. I don't think Mama could do much good in Grams' eyes and looking back I never saw them hug, kiss, or say a kind word to each other too many times. Most conversations centered on what we were going to eat and so forth. The eating part was mostly about Sunday dinner. It is clear to me now, I got all the love that Mama and Roxie never did.

J.W. finally made his appearance at the house and I think it was love at first sight for me. He picked me up in his arms, twirled me around like Mr. Willard did, and gave me a hug that was so warm and tight that it was almost frightening. As much as Grams loved me, her age kept her from picking me up. John William and Mama headed out for their first of many dates to the drive-in movie and I was left to dream that he would be my daddy someday.

J.W. wanted to spend time with me so he took me out one night with him and Mama. Where else would we go but to the drive-in movie? In the 1950s cars had front seats that completely folded down and there were no seat belts, airbags, or seats that would lock in place. I was sitting in the back seat when J.W. had to come to a quick stop and the momentum threw me towards the front of the car and my face slammed into the back of the seat. J.W looked back with concern and asked if I was alright.

"Lord, don't let anything happen to her!" Mama said in a loud voice. "My mama would have a hissy fit."

"Yor mama? What about you?" J.W. said to her.

There it was. Another sign. Mama had said she loved me once, wasn't going to give me up to my daddy, but just made it clear that I was more important to someone else than to her. Life just got more confusing. I thought Mama was the one who was supposed to love me more than anyone.

A few months after Mama and J.W. started dating, my Aunt Roxie, Uncle Austin, and my cousins had all come down from Chicago for a visit and there was a picnic for everyone at the church. I had three cousins, Cid, the oldest, Suzanne and Lisa by order of age. Melanie was on the way. They all piled into a car together except for Lisa and me. I was sick and Lisa too young to go. Grams stayed home to take care of Lisa and me. Mama was in the front seat with Uncle Austin driving so Suzanne and Cid were in the back with Aunt Roxie. They were less than a mile from the house when a car, driven by a drunk driver, swerved and hit them head on. Mama, with potato salad in her lap, went through the windshield and came back to the inside of the car. Tempered glass was either not invented or not being used yet, so the glass broke into shards. Jagged edges of non-tempered glass, used at this time cut Mama all around her face.

Mama was taken by ambulance to a hospital in Athens, over a half hour away. We were all waiting for Mama since Uncle Austin had called from the hospital and said she would be alright. None of us was prepared to see Mama as she got out of the car. Her head was bandaged except for the holes that allowed her to see, breath, and talk. Seeing the red spots oozing through the gauze bandage scared me even more. Everyone said she would be alright but I wasn't sure.

"Oh my Lord, Jessie!" Grams was shocked as well and scurried off to get Mama some iced tea.

Georgia sweet tea cured anything but by the small chance it didn't, a tablespoon of sugar filled with whiskey would do the trick.

When we saw dust rising from the road and a police siren we knew it was J.W. Since he was a state police officer, he heard about it on the radio but didn't know it was Mama right away. By the time he found out, she was already at home. He drove that state police car as fast as he could to our house. He ran through the yard as if the house was on fire trying to get to the woman he adored. The screen door flew open and his eyes found Mama immediately. He almost broke down in tears seeing Mama's bandaged head but choked the tears back as he took hold of her hand.

"Thank Gawd you are alright. I love you so much."

He went on to explain how he heard it over the police radio and told his captain he had to go.

It took Mama a month or so to heal and J.W. proposed soon after. Mama said yes with all the zeal she could muster. It was a small wedding, no long white dress or fancy cake and it was held at Grams' house. There were just a few people in attendance including myself all dressed up with white shoes, gloves and a hat, just like Mama and Grams. Grams liked J.W. just about as much as she could like any man. It was such a happy day and I felt my life was going to be complete, just like all the other kids with two parents. I didn't know it would mean leaving Grams. They hadn't told me yet.

J.W. was being transferred to Gainesville, Georgia, which was about an hour and a half north of Bishop, but light years from Grams, the person who held my heart. Being told we were moving north, I asked if we were going where people sounded like Yankees. That was the only time we all laughed about going away. I could see concern in Grams' face and hear it in her voice, feel it when the hugs were so intense I thought I might suffocate. How would we make it without each other? I felt she was the only family who loved me and could show it. Mama never hugged me and most times I was just a bother to her. This was never intentional on her part but only because she was incapable of the emotion it took to show love for an extended period. She didn't have a problem with short bursts of passion; but, she was powerless to sustain it, as J.W. would learn.

Moving day came too soon. As I looked from the back window of the car at Grams waving goodbye and throwing kisses, I knew those kisses were for only me and no one else. I sobbed almost uncontrollably as she got smaller and smaller the further we drove away. Like Alice in Wonderland.

"She always looks where we've been and not where we're goin'. I hope she won't do that when she's older." J.W. was very perceptive.

The move was hard and I thought the hardest part was leaving Grams, until I started school. I was a good student, smart and well-mannered as I had been taught. Respect your elders, don't talk back, and never roll your eyes. There was not one kid in my class from divorced parents, no one else with a stepfather. There was one Jewish fella which was uncommon in itself in the South, but still I had many questions being constantly asked of me.

We had joined a church right away and soon afterwards there was a pot luck dinner one Sunday night in the basement of the church. The Pastor introduced us as Mr. and Mrs. Cobb and their daughter, Carol Saxon. People started to whisper, but not in a mean way, just a curious one, like first contact with a primitive tribe. My parents had to explain immediately that Mama was divorced and I was her child, and J.W's stepchild.

"What does it mean that your mama's divorced?"

"What is a stepdad like? Is he mean?"

"Why don't you have the same last name as your mom and dad?"

"Why don't you have any brothers or sisters?"

The questions kept coming and for a second I thought it was because people thought I was special but come to find out, we were different. The only divorced, stepdad, stepchild, not the same last name, no brothers or sisters family in the group. Not only had I been taken out of Bishop but I had been tossed into another world where there was no familiarity. Being an only child didn't help either since that was also an anomaly. It seems so strange now to think someone could be different being from a divorced family when it has become the norm today. I finally did make some friends and most of them were children of other state police officers with parents who had the same last name and brothers or sisters. Since Mama and J.W. both worked full time, they hired a young black woman to be home with me after school. I had been raised right by my Grams and knew what priorities were; doing my homework as soon as I got home, being polite to all adults, and following the Ten Commandments and the Golden Rule. Easy. Therefore, there wasn't much need for interaction between me and the young girl, so I mostly kept to myself and she did the same until Mama came home from work to relieve Sissy of her guard duties.

I loved J.W. like a real father although I always called him by his name, and never "Daddy." I decided early on that either I wouldn't have a daddy or no one would be around long enough to deserve the title. However, since I had no connection with Edd, J.W. meant the world to me. At least he would try to discipline me while Mama would allow me to do anything, but that meant he cared. Mama was wrapped up in her own head and it was sometimes hard for her to unclasp her mind.  Already I could see that Mama didn't give hugs to J.W. either. Every time he came home, he went straight to her, put his arms around her and gave her a kiss, sometimes wanting to linger for a bit. My mother's idea of a hug was putting one arm behind your shoulder and patting you three times. The other hand was usually holding a cigarette or a cup of coffee. Even as a child, I knew he wanted and needed more from Mama so I tried to love him with all my might, hugging him tight when he reached out for me after Mama's three pats.

After being in Gainesville for about three years, J.W. was in his state patrol car with another officer who had become his best friend. A big industrial crane was on the side of the road where a new building was in progress and somehow the crane came down on top of the patrol car. The car flipped upside down and caught on fire. People were all around the construction site and ran to them while someone called the ambulances. J.W. and his partner were pulled from the car before it exploded, like a movie, but it was real life.

I knew something was wrong when a neighbor picked me up from school instead of Mama but she showed up shortly after. It was still hard to read Mama since she didn't show much emotion or feelings about too many things. She would just smoke more and drink more coffee. The neighbor and Mama whispered as I tried to listen in. Mama told me about the accident and J.W.'s severe head injury.

"Is he gonna be alright, Mama?" I was terrified.

"I don't know, Carol. We'll see."

J.W.'s parents lived about an hour away on a country road  in a town called Bogart but I'm not sure why it even had a name. Their house sat about three miles down a red clay road and

J.W.'s grandparents who were about a hundred lived two miles from them on the same red clay road. The red Georgia clay turned your hands and feet, clothes, hair and whatever else it meets RED. They had lived in the same house on the same road for their entire lives. A car came by only once a week or so and you could see it coming for miles. Everyone would immediately start to close the windows in the house and wait for it to come back by before opening them again. Since it was the only road in and out of the woods we knew it would be back shortly. The only other people who lived on that road were J.W.'s grandparents, so these outsiders had no business on the road and someone in J.W.'s family would eventually look for them and chase them away. There was no running water at the house but water was scooped up from a fresh running stream three times a day to fill a bucket. An outhouse served for a bathroom with a *pee pot* in your room at night. All the cooking was done on a cast iron wood burning stove and the farm went on for acres and acres. Hen houses meant fresh eggs every morning and the beef and hogs provided meat for the family. I remember several times when the five or six dogs that ran the grounds would tangle with wild dogs or wild hogs and come home bloody and torn. J.W.'s father put coal tar on their wounds to heal them. The coal tar smelled like blacktop or roofing tar. It was an old remedy that was used for years on animals and livestock. There was no TV but they did have a phone.

J.W.'s family was at our house very soon. I feigned sleep as the adults whispered about the situation. I heard them say it would be best for everyone that I go to the red clay road and stay with J.W.'s parents. I learned now not to listen to whispers. Maybe if I didn't move for a long time they wouldn't bother me and I could stay with Mama. But no, they decided to wake me up and tell me I had to stay at the red clay road house for two weeks while Mama concentrated on J.W. As much as I was worried about him, I hated the fact I had to stay at that house with no one around for miles and nothing to do.

Trying to keep me busy and my mind off things, J.W.'s parents had me pickin' peanuts, shellin' peas, getting the daily drinking water from the stream (which I remember today as the coldest, best water I have ever had) and gathering the eggs. We went to see the cows and bulls sometimes, too. It wasn't as bad as I thought but I still couldn't wait to go home.

This should have been the perfect time for me to go and stay with Grams. I asked to stay with her but Mama said it was too far and Grams wasn't feeling up to it. She was aging and getting ailments peculiar to old people. There was no one to take care or look after her anymore. She had visited us a couple of times and bought a piano for me. It was her dream that I would learn to play like the girl on *The Lawrence Welk Show*. I pretended not to like going to practice, but secretly I loved it but couldn't tell anyone. No kid wants their parents to know they like something they were made to do.

After a few weeks, J.W. was allowed home from the hospital which meant I could go home, too. He had lost weight and there was a different look in his coal black eyes. It was fear, easy for even a child to pick up. He started having nightmares and Mama and I would startle awake with his screaming. It was always the same with him sitting backwards in a kitchen chair simulating a car seat, I suppose, and yelling "we're on fire" over and over.

"Help us, help us."

Mama would shake him and tell him to wake up. She was annoyed that her sleep was interrupted and told him he needed to do something about it. It didn't matter what time of day or night. If Mama had to get up for anything, even to go to the bathroom, she would light a cigarette and make coffee.

Mama was not good at dealing with tragedies and with even the small ones, she acted as if the world was ending. I got that from her and continue to fight that feeling of desperation and foreboding. She really didn't know how to deal with J.W. She was emotionally distraught most of the time and no one or nothing could soothe her except cigarettes and coffee. Desperation, extreme anxiety, worry, nervousness were all words that described Mama day in and day out.

The State would not let J.W. go back to work for almost a year so he got a job selling insurance. He drove to the customer's house and talked to them face to face. It was summer and I went along with him many times and felt so wanted again. I loved it and hoped it wouldn't end. People always offered sweet tea and sandwiches or pie depending on the time of day. Spending that time with him was exactly what I wanted and I felt almost grateful for the accident that brought us together. I was getting attention and felt loved but it wouldn't replace Grams.

Chapter 4

*My J.W.*

J.W.'s physical and mental wounds from the accident healed and he was reinstated at the Georgia State Patrol. That was good news but along with it came the bad. He was being transferred to Swainsboro, Georgia, a place I had never heard of and once again, seemed too far away. It was in the southern part of the state and hours away from Grams. I was ten years old.

We moved into an apartment that was longer than it was wide. There were three dwellings with one behind the other and we were in the last of them. The building was made of stucco, inside and out, and we became aware of this the first day of ninety degree weather. Mama and I came home to walls that had water lines running from top to bottom and were wet to the touch. It was akin to a horror movie, something Hitchcock would use, and it rattled us both. Mama called the landlord and told him, breathlessly, what we were looking at.

"Mr. Jenkins, the walls are all wet. What's happened here? Why, I've neva seen anythin' like it! You betta get ova here before J.W. gets home!"

He calmly told her that the building was stucco which would "sweat" unless there was cool air circulating inside. Sweating walls? We had never lived in southern Georgia before this and obviously had things to learn about life in hot and humid weather. From then on we ran rotating fans throughout the house to solve the problem. Southern Georgia was much different than the north. No red clay but sand instead.

The great thing I liked about the apartment was it had a cement walkway all the way around the long building which made for a perfect place to roller skate. Not rollerblade, but skate with metal adjustable skates that had a key to change the size of the metal base that would hold your shoe. I rolled 'round and 'round hours at a time. When I wasn't skating, I was collecting snails, which were in great abundance from the humidity. They went into my red wagon with a bed of grass inside for them to eat. Most likely they died in there, since I never took them out. The most fun was when J.W. would take me into the yard and give me lessons on how to throw a fishing line. He was so proud of the how far I could toss it.

"As good as any boy" he would say.

We would go fishing as a family which meant J.W. and I would fish, and Mama would sit on the bank smoking one cigarette after another complaining all the while that she sure would like some coffee. Occasionally, J.W. would call to her to look at how good I could throw the fishing line which was addressed with an "um hum" and the lighting of another cigarette. Mama didn't know how to enjoy life being so wrapped up in her own mind.

There were some times when I really need to have a mother to talk to but had to really talk myself into to doing it. For example, when I was eleven, I thought I was dying. I found a knot or lump in my chest and had no idea what it could be. After debating with myself for several days, I finally decided to tell Mama. I would have told Grams right away if she had been there but I was afraid that Mama wouldn't know what to do. I pulled her into the bathroom and opened my blouse, prepared for the worst. Mama felt the knot and started to laugh.

"Carol, you're just growin' breasts! Wait till I tell Mama!" she said.

I felt relieved and realized I was growing up and could get a bra. Wow! I might have been one of the first in my class. Then it happened.

"J.W. come quick and look at Carol's bosom!"

How could she! J.W. came to the bathroom with a look of horror on his face. Mama told him to feel the lump and he refused.

"I'm not going to do that" he said emphatically. "Carol, button your blouse!"

"Oh, J.W., don't be so silly. All little girls go through it. It's normal! She's just going to be wearing a bra now. Look at it"!

I could not believe my ears and to have J.W. standing in front of me just as embarrassed was living hell.

He walked away and Mama stood shaking her head while I got the hell out of the bathroom and couldn't look at J.W. for days. In a few days Mama and I went bra shopping and once again pointed it out to J.W. that I had to wear a bra now. I hoped that was the end of it all and it was. I needed to build a wall to protect me from Mama.

We stayed in the sweating walls place for a short time more and then rented a house that was near a small cliff or drop off corner where a road had been cut through. Mama was working at the local Ford Motor Company as a secretary. She was still a looker and J.W. was quite jealous but Mama took pleasure in telling him the stories of how many men had asked her out during the day. You could see his anger in those dark eyes and he would make a comment about how he didn't like it, but never would he lose control or show anger further than a comment. Again, I would witness the unsuccessful attempts by J.W. to get affection from Mama. She was content with talking about what other men might want of her rather than having a close relationship with her husband. She just couldn't feel.

The 1960s racial wars were in full swing, which meant the Georgia Patrol worked long hours and was often in the middle of riots and arson. It was definitely a time of worry for everyone and I could tell Mama was worried when J.W. would work twelve- or fourteen-hour days. The later it got the more she smoked and drank coffee. A hundred degrees outside and in and she drank coffee.

I was old enough to worry, too, and I couldn't wait for him to come home. About this time J.W. started letting me clean his uniform badge which was the same number as a famous detective on a TV show, *Dragnet*: Jack Webb, badge number 714. We used Brasso to polish up the brass and it shined like the sun.

After he emptied his gun and put the bullets away, I was allowed to clean that and then his belt buckle. Being on the Georgia State Patrol was a bit like being in the military as far as always having the perfect uniform. The hat was hard brimmed with a small tassel in the front. The uniform was grey wool and no one was more handsome in it that my step father. The hat hid his baldness, which directed your attention to those coal black eyes.

One morning we woke up and the front wheels of the patrol car were precariously hanging over the drop off. J.W. warned us not to go near it as he called his commander. A big wrecker came and was able to get all four wheels back on solid ground but the mystery was how it got there in the first place. The ground was level and the car locked. The conclusion was that someone had managed to push it to the cliff and must have gotten scared or been seen and left. If the car had been pushed off, it could have killed a passerby. There were lots of things being done to officers during this tumultuous time. Black people hated white people, white people hated black people, and the wars waged every day. Everyone was afraid even walking down the street.

Growing up in a race war does different things to different people. You can become very hateful and prejudiced or compassionate and caring. I took the latter route because of my Grams and my Christian upbringing, I suppose. I don't feel I've ever been prejudiced and would get a stern look or switchin' if I ever said a mean word about anyone when Grams was around. J.W.'s attitude was that he had a job to do, and at home he always set a good example. He was the one in our household that the adults in the neighborhood talked to the most. My mama mostly kept to herself but never knew a stranger. She could carry on a conversation with anyone as long as it wasn't about feelings. She had a quick Irish wit and could snap a comeback to a comment as quick as you could snap your fingers. Everybody liked Mama.

A couple of years went by and I made some good friends. One of them told me their parents were selling their house so I mentioned it at home. Soon we were moving in to our own little three bedroom all brick house. There was room in the backyard for dog kennels so J.W. bought a couple of huntin' dogs and Mama hated them. Mama didn't want to be bothered by outside sources such as cats, dogs, or humans unless it was a handsome man who paid her attention. She just couldn't help herself, the feelings she had or didn't have. J.W. was so happy with those dogs and his attention went directly to them went he came home from work. By now he had discovered the inevitable: he would get no attention from Mama and it was starting to put a wedge into all of our relationships. We never used the word *family* to describe the three of us and it was just as well since we wouldn't survive as one. Besides that, I knew in my heart that a family was forever.

In order to appease Mama somewhat J.W. came up with a compromise for her. She would get a washer and dryer and an upright freezer and he could keep the dogs. The freezer—the one with the big drawer on the bottom—was for the game he brought home from hunting with his dogs. He bragged that he paid for good pointin' dogs and he sure got 'em. That was a temporary truce between them but then Grams came to live with us. She's become too ill to care for herself. I understood she was sick but I don't think I understood what it meant. I was just pleased to see that there was a young black girl who stayed with her during the day and was there for me when I came home from school. Her name was Ramee and she was young enough that we could converse with each other. My friends sometimes came home after school with me and we would stand in the hallway next to Grams' room and laugh ourselves sick. The old people sounds that came from that room were too much for anyone to keep a straight face. After that, we would sneak out the back door and smoke a cigarette. Ramee asked if Mama knew I was doing that and I told her no and please don't tell. She said she wouldn't and never did and it didn't worry me much. What did make me worry was Grams finding out. I couldn't bear to do anything that would hurt her or especially make her feel disappointed in me. We couldn't really inhale those cigarettes without coughing up a lung so we just gave up. At the Five and Dime with my friends one day, we were all given a dare by a schoolmate to steal something, anything, to prove we could get away with it. I took a pair of underwear and stuffed it under my blouse, just like everyone else. We all laughed and joked about how cool it was while patting each other on the back. I went home by myself, went directly out the backdoor, tossed the panties in the garbage and threw up. I prayed God would forgive me and knew if we had been back in Bishop, I would be picking a switch. The guilt wouldn't leave me for days and I could barely look Grams in the eye.

Mama had to take time off work to get Grams to her doctor's appointments. You could tell it was bothering her to do so but at the same time she felt obligated. I thought Mama loved Grams but neither of them knew how to show affection to the other. J.W. was very tolerant of the whole situation and always treated Grams with respect and admiration. Grams stayed in her bed all the time so sometimes I sat and read to her, just like she read to me when I was little. I could see her health failing but her mind remained sharp as a tack. I had no doubt that if she could get up from that bed she would have whipped my behind with a switch many times. Because she was sick I tried my best to stay on track, but without having much discipline from anywhere else it was becoming increasingly more difficult. Hormones were running rampant through my body and there was no one to tell me how to deal with them. My friends and I would talk about it but they were no more informed than I was so we all just made up stuff. In the early 1960s there was still a large puritanical society and things such as sex were never discussed by anyone. We would spend afternoons in the hot sun trying to figure out what you did to have sex. When one of the girls said the penis went into the woman, we were all so grossed out that we thought we would NEVER let that happen to us. So we just danced.

\*\*\*

I was twelve and news came again of another transfer for J.W. This time to a town called Thomson; the beginning of the end.

J.W got a temporary apartment in Thomson but came back on his days off. Mama told me Grams was getting worse and that it was hard for her to take care of Grams with us moving to Thomson. Mama decided to put Grams in a nursing home and I was heartbroken knowing the person who loved me the most would be out of my life again. Thank goodness I had J.W. but he wasn't showing me as much affection as he used to. I thought he was just busy and I was getting older so maybe I shouldn't expect so much.

We got Grams moved into a nursing home in Athens, near Bishop where we had lived. This allowed her neighbors to visit but would be hours away from us. It took a couple of months to sell the house and J.W. had rented a very large house for us in the new town. Soon we were all packed up and moving away. It was just when school had ended so I would have the entire summer without any friends. Luckily we had a neighbor with two girls and one was my age. We became friends in a short time so I was feeling ok about things.

Mama had not found a job but we were sure it would be soon. She did her last job extremely well and had been loved by all of her peers. Her personality was suited to dealing with the public since she never knew a stranger and could talk about anything. At least she was that way at work. Being at home was a different story and she wanted to keep to herself with her two best friends, coffee and cigarettes. We would ask her to fish with us, play cards with us, and watch TV with us but none of it was of interest to her. She did have a tendency to walk a lot and I think that partly came from the fact that she didn't like to drive. Mechanical things were a puzzle to Mama and even changing a light bulb was difficult. I say this not as sarcasm or a joke but the truth was she just didn't want to or know how to deal with mundane things. It was a marvel she could use a typewriter but managed that somehow and maybe it was because she learned in school and it was just part of her job. She told me many times that she loved math because "it was the only thing that didn't lie." She was never a good cook but nonetheless put food on the table every night. J.W. bought her a pressure cooker thinking it would help hone her skills and be easier for her. The first time she used it, she was cooking greens and the lid blew off and hit the ceiling. We had to clean turnip greens off the walls and ceiling for days and J.W. casually remarked how lucky we were that no one had their head blown off. Poor Mama. At lease she had really tried.

Soon J.W. was spending less time at home even when he was off work. I noticed he had stopped trying to hug Mama at all anymore, like he had given up. Of course our relationship was strained, as well. It was also evident that Mama was becoming more anxious, smoking constantly, not sleeping, and chewing her nails, making coffee in the middle of the night when he wasn't home. I woke up during the night sometimes to the clanging sound of the coffee cup being cradled in the saucer. The smell of smoke filled the house as Mama smoked one after another.

One night after dark, she asked me to go with her for a ride. Back then, people would just drive around waving at the other people doing the same. Up and down the same highway usually. But on this night she veered off to a side road. She was very nervous and I wasn't sure what was going on but J.W. was on patrol. She drove slowly by a house I wasn't familiar with and said she thought J.W.'s car might be there. Though I did not understand why we were doing this, Mama said she just had an idea. About what, I wondered. We kept driving when suddenly Mama spotted a patrol car at a pay phone booth. They were on almost every corner and gas station. She became disturbed and told me to quickly see if it was J.W. in the phone booth. As we drove by, I could tell it was him because I knew the number on his patrol car. Once I told Mama it was him, she handed me a piece of paper with a phone number and at the next phone booth told me to dial the number. I got out of the car and did what I was told, all the while not sure what was happening. The line was busy. Someone was talking and I couldn't get through to the stranger I had been asked to call. Looking at Mama I shook my head and told her. She became more wound up and agitated so we went directly home. We must have looked like we were on fire as the smoke from her cigarettes filled the space behind us as we drove towards home.

About an hour later J.W. came home from work. Mama was waiting for him, for the opportunity to confront him with what she knew was true. She said she knew he had called a woman but he denied it and did his part by acting surprised that she could even think such a terrible thing. The blowout continued until he admitted he had been seeing someone. A woman he had met soon after he transferred to Thomson. He told Mama she was cold, uncaring, and that he wanted children of his own. I had never heard any talk about babies but I had wanted a sibling my entire life. Most only children do, I thought. It was over and there was no doubt about it. Mama was incapable of showing love to not only me, but to anyone in her life. The rock group The Eagles had a song called "Desperado." A lyric in the song reads "Your prison is walking through this world all alone." I've heard this song dozens or maybe hundreds of times in my life and always I think of Mama. After all, you can still be alone in a room full of people.

Things progressed quickly and J.W. was gone the next day. The woman he met had five children and she and J.W. had a child within a year. We had been together as a family for about six years and only in Thomson for less than three months. We were going back to Swainsboro, just Mama and me. Grams was in the nursing home and not doing very well.

Mama was able to get her old job back at the Ford place and we rented a small two-bedroom apartment. It was once the slave quarters of the property owners who lived in front of us. Not unusual for the South, a lot of slave quarters were turned into apartments like ours. Mama became even more distant and distraught but capable of doing the great job that was expected of her at the Ford place. I was in my early teens and came home from school to be by myself. At the time, I was a good kid and did my homework with no coaxing or instruction. Mama and I would go out for dinner most every night since she thought it was crazy to cook for just two. Most of the time we went to a nearby hotel that had a restaurant and my favorite was vegetable soup and a grilled cheese sandwich. This was my dinner four nights out of seven. Mama had a light dinner but always with coffee and cigarettes. If the smoking ban had been in force back in those days, Mama probably would have broken the law a million times.

The first Christmas with J.W. being gone, I heard a strange noise coming from Mama's room. As I slowly opened the door I could see she was crying. This was a strange sight for me and I'm not sure I had seen it before. So surprised at the sight, I wondered what had happened and what to do. After all, Mama didn't cry.

"Mama, Mama, what's happened? Is Grams alright?" Starting to let my mind wander, I was getting scared.

"I just miss J.W., Carol."

 What? Did I hear that right? Remorse and feelings coming from Mama were much more than I expected. Would I be getting a hug now? I reached out to comfort her and she got up from the bed, said "I'll be alright," lit a cigarette, and went on her way.

She came home from work, we went to dinner, and she repaired to her room while I was left to watch TV or talk on the phone with friends. There wasn't much life going on for either of us; just day in and day out, always the same. At least we would take a trip to see Grams once in a while. Once she decided to drive to Atlanta to see relatives and it was when the freeways were first being built. We got close to Atlanta and there it was, straight ahead, the freeway.

"Oh Lord" said Mama, "I don't know how to drive on one of those things."

The proof of that statement came quickly as she turned onto the freeway going the wrong way. Luckily, not many cars were using it yet so the amount of horns blowing wasn't as deafening as it would be today. It didn't take much to persuade her to pull over and let me drive even though I was only fourteen. J.W. had taught me to drive while I sat in his lap. It was his parents' old car and it was a four speed (not much else back then) and he taught me how to shift gears and be a defensive driver. Whenever we would visit the house on the red clay road, I knew it was my chance to drive and it was what I looked forward to. Therefore, we made it to Atlanta and back, with me driving, safe and sound.

After working for awhile, Mama was making more money and we were able to rent a house. It was off the main drag where all the teenagers drove their cars up and down the street to Sam's restaurant/drive-in. Sam's was THE hangout and you were cool if you went there. That would come a little later for me as I wasn't quite the age yet. Two blocks from our house down on Main Street, there was a little store. Mama would have me walk down there to buy her cigarettes and coffee or whatever little things we needed. Even a kid could buy smokes. When I turned fifteen, I talked her into letting me drive the Dodge the two blocks to the store to "get driving practice." The time had come when it was too much for Mama to deal with me so I did just about anything I wanted. No daddy, no Grams, no J.W. made it easy to be bad.

## Chapter 5

*Fifteen and Pregnant*

School started up again and I fell into my old group of friends since I was only gone the summer months. I was fourteen and hormones were raging like wildfires. Boy crazy was the word used to describe someone like me. Even though it was a tender age, I hungered for the excitement of having a boy kissing me and doing other things, as well. I wasn't sure what that was but I knew it was something not talked about. Mama never talked to me about any of the birds and bees so I would have to find out for myself.

She was letting me drive the car more and more even though I was only fourteen. She just wanted peace and quiet in the house and if I wasn't there she didn't have to deal with me. Sam's drive-in was my first stop every night when I left the house. Sam's wasn't a drive-in movie but a drive-in food place. Cars pulled into diagonal stalls and a roller-skating waitress came to the car to take your order. She brought it back on a tray that hung over the slightly rolled up car window but the smell of the hotdogs and fries couldn't overcome the smell of the car exhausts. None of us really cared about the food. It was a place to hang out, be cool, smoke cigarettes, drink moonshine and homemade wine, and throw up on occasion. Fast cars. They went around and around like horses on a carousel. Boys revving engines, using the sound as a mating call. We jumped in one car for a ride, and then another. Several different ones in a night. Sometimes we had no idea who the boys were but they had a cool car.

Each time I went to Sam's I would stay a little longer so Mama figured out what I was doing. She wasn't really mad that I was going to Sam's but more upset that she had to do without a cigarette or coffee for five minutes. I was scolded and told that I had to come straight home. No fooling around. I knew there were no consequences so I kept circling 'round and 'round letting the boys know I was available. Let a dog off its leash and it'll run till you catch it.

At fifteen, one of my friends was dating a boy and they asked me to double date with his cousin, Ronnie. He was an outsider which interested me since all the boys in town were getting rather boring. I drove the Dodge out to Sam's to meet the three of them. Pulling up beside them, I looked in the backseat and there he was. It was lust at first sight. Alrighty then! I crawled into the backseat and we took off down the road for our date. Ronnie was about five foot teen  with a small, toned build, and bleached blond hair in the bowl cut style of the Beatles. The heat we were feeling wasn't coming from the night, but from two teenage bodies a-blazin'. There were so many hormones between the four of us there must have been steam coming out the windows. We drove around Sam's a few times and then up and down the road, back around Sam's and on and on. Since we hit it off so well, basically being all hot and bothered, we decided to go out the next weekend. Mama didn't think any of this was a good idea but once I told her the other girls were doing it, she thought for sure it must be fine.

We went to the record hop, a dance held in a warehouse with a his-and-hers bathroom and a few folding chairs around the outside walls, for the wall flowers. Vinyl records were played by the local radio DJ, who was our only town celebrity. We danced the shag, the stroll, the twist, the pony, and all the others we learned from watching *American Bandstand*. Things were getting hot so we left early to go parking. Yes, you took your parked car and drove it to a place to park. A secluded place, a dark place, and a lot of neckin' which meant kissin' and whatever else, a lot of feeling up. My friend and her boyfriend lay in the front seat while Ronnie and I lay down in the back. Our hands were in constant motion, as if they were motorized and couldn't be turned off. Our lips were so wet with teen passion that we were both aching to do the deed. But with the couple in the front seat, we put it off and lived in agony for the next week until we had a date with just the two of us.

Friday night came and all I thought about during the week was Ronnie, night and day. Being a good student was even more of a responsibility now since I spent my free time daydreaming about him. He came to the house and met Mama. She and I were in the kitchen alone and the only thing she said in an excited voice was "Carol, he's cute!" We left the house and went to Sam's. It was an unspoken rule that no matter what you were going to do you had to drive through Sam's before and after. We rode up and down the main drag for a while, both of us nervous and knowing what we truly wanted from each other. We found our dark place to park and in the back seat of his souped-up Chevy he said "Do you want to?" I let him know with my wet kisses and hot, sweaty, sticky body that there was no doubt of the answer. So it happened and I fell in love instantly. I was fifteen; he was sixteen.

Ronnie lived in a town about an hour and a half from Swainsboro. He had dropped out and started driving to Swainsboro every day to pick me up from school. Sometimes we would go to my house since Mama was at work but I was a little concerned about the neighbors telling Mama I was alone in the house with a boy. If they did, I was pretty sure not much would happen. She would ask if we were doing anything we shouldn't be, I would say no, and she would say ok. Just the same, we started going to the drive-in movie. Of course, it wasn't open during the day so behind the big screen made a great parking place.

The speakers were the only witness to our love making in the back seat of Ronnie's car, and it became our place day after day. He could barely get the car turned off before we were getting out of our clothes. Passion filled the air and there was no one in the world but the two of us. I fell in love with Ronnie and, being so sure he was in love with me, I wanted to have his baby. I knew for sure that if I got pregnant, Ronnie and I would live happily ever after, just like the fairy tales. Always wanting a family, I knew this was the way to get it. I told Ronnie that having a baby would keep us together forever and our parents could do nothing about it. He showed every sign he agreed with me. That night it happened. I'm sure it was that night because no one in the world had ever wanted a baby more than me.

Mama was wrapped up in her job and came home to her coffee and cigarettes every day. She would ask if my homework was done, which it always was, and about Ronnie. Mama had no idea about the after-school movie! She really started to like Ronnie and they would talk about the weather and such when he was at the house. Of course, she did ask him about his parents. Not that she really wanted to know but it was the right thing to do. Sometimes Mama did things because she knew they were expected of her and not because she really had an interest. Both of his parents worked and made good money. Mama said that was good.

As the weeks passed, Ronnie took me to meet his parents. I was welcomed into their home and felt good about the decision we had made. They would make terrific grandparents! I was so tiny that my pregnancy didn't show until I was almost seven months and I could hide it easily with clothes. Ronnie and I continued our love making but the passion was wearing off for him and he started going out with other girls. Soon he stopped coming to see me and didn't call. I felt like a mess and had no one to turn to. Telling Grams would kill her and I didn't feel safe enough or close enough to any friends or Mama to let them know. Without even knowing, Mama had taught me to keep things to myself. Don't ask for help, just bottle it up and have a nervous breakdown. I had to keep going to school as if nothing had changed and pretend every day that I was just like everyone else. Inside I was dying and crying to myself. Months went by and no one knew except Ronnie and me.

Because Ronnie had started to drift away from me I wrote him a letter and reminded him of our bond, and my pregnancy. Wondering if he had told his parents and if he was just pretending that everything was normal too, I pleaded with him to visit me.

The next week I heard his car drive up at the house. I opened the front door as he was getting out.

"I can tell," he said, meaning he could see his baby in my small body.

Without delay he told me that his dad, James, had suspected something all along and steamed open the letter. He knew and now it was up to us to tell our mothers. Ronnie didn't stay long but went back home to confess to both his parents, but it would take him several days to get the courage.

In the meantime, I was called to the counselor's office at school because they had noticed the small bump, since I was almost eight months. They asked if my mama knew. I hung my head and said no, as the tears started to flow. I was in so much trouble, I thought. How did it all happen? How could I be so stupid to think a boy could love me forever? Nobody could love me for long except Grams. Now they all would know and I would be the laughing stock of the school. The whispers in the hallway had already started and I hated myself with everything on this earth. I didn't have the guts to tell Mama so the school said they would do it for me. Now what? It was a major catastrophe.

I left school shaking, wanting to throw up and cleanse myself of the evil I had done. Nobody was ever going to like me again and Grams would die if she knew her precious child she loved so much had created such tragedy. Mama worked just a few blocks away and I had driven the car to school. She was waiting for me with cigarette in hand and taking one deep drag after another. "Let's go out to Sam's" she said acting like it was a normal day. But we both knew it wasn't, yet each of us screamed silently in our own heads and knew reality was about to hit us head on. That day I became an island sitting alone in the middle of nowhere. People may have been around me but I was never with them. I was drifting.

Once there, Mama straight out asked if I was pregnant. Finally breaking down and sobbing I told her yes, and she never asked who the father was. She knew. I had not seen anyone since

Ronnie. "It'll be alright, Carol. This isn't the first or last time this has happened to anybody. It'll be alright." It was obvious to me she was trying to comfort herself as much as she was me. She was as afraid as I was. Mama was not comfortable touching or being touched but I knew she felt pity for me.

"Can I have a cigarette?"

"Have you been smoking?" Mama asked.

"Yes."

So Mama gave me a Winston and we sat at Sam's, both staring straight ahead into the bright sunny day, sharing a smoke for the first time. How do such bad things happen on such beautiful days, I wondered. We had the closest feelings toward each other that day than we had felt in a long time, but it was temporary.

In a few days Ronnie and family were at our house. There was no doubt what was going to happen, it was just when and where. Grace and James, Ronnie's parents, had planned the future for us.

"Ronnie, do you love Carol?" Grace asked.

"Yes."

"Carol, do you love Ronnie"

"Yes."

"Well, I've always believed things happen for a reason and they do love each other. They can get married at the courthouse here and move in with us. I'm sure it would be easier for you, too, Jessie, having them with us since you are alone and work so much." Grace was being polite.

Down to the courthouse we went, on the very same day. We were told we had to wait three days for blood tests, but life was so simple then. "She's fifteen and pregnant" were all the words it took to get things moving like a freight train. We were married within a few minutes.

I packed up my clothes, said goodbye to Mama, and went to my new home excited that Ronnie and I were finally together forever and my dream was coming true. Mama was smoking up a storm and said the usual "don't worry, Carol. It'll be alright." Three pats on the back from Mama and we were gone.

Moving in with the new family didn't seem so bad, at first. James did most of the cooking and he and Grace worked opposite shifts with Ronnie working overnight so there was always someone home. I was weeks away from giving birth, at sixteen, and had never seen a doctor. Grace found one that accepted me as a patient.

It wasn't long and the day came when my water broke. I had no idea what was happening until Grace told me. She acted like I was stupid and should have known what to do but I was sixteen. The doctor put me in a room by myself and occasionally a nurse would check on me. There was no one there, not Grace, James, Ronnie, or Mama. Unlike today, no one was allowed in the room with me. They gave me a drug that made me sleepy but I looked down towards my legs and saw blood. I was screaming in pain and just knew I was going to die, bleed to death was my assumption. A nurse walked briskly into my room and raised her voice over mine and told me to shut up and be quiet."You are just having a baby," she said. They gave me more drugs to shut me up and when I woke up I had given birth to a girl. James was sitting in my room but no one else was there. Grace told me Ronnie was out celebrating with his friends. He had come into the hospital while I was still comatose from drugs and looked at our baby through a window. The hospital stay was three days and I saw Ronnie once. Mama said she was busy with work and would come later. I knew she didn't want to drive that far and understood her hesitation; she was such a bad driver. Grace came as often as she could and was the most excited of anyone, telling me how she could take care of things when we got home.

I named our baby Shelia Lynn. Naming her was the only thing I had control over.

Home came soon enough and Grace held the baby all the way during the car ride. Sheila Lynn was beautiful but she would never belong to me. Grace and James were thrilled to be grandparents and neither Ronnie nor I knew what to think about it. We didn't have to think about it much since Grace and James thought about it all the time. Their family and friends were called to come to the house and see their grandbaby. Sometimes I was lucky enough to get introduced as being the child's mother but, of course, her son Ronnie was the father. Grace had once asked Ronnie if he was sure he was the father and he answered his mother with a stern "Hell, yeah."

There was plenty of room in the new house Ronnie's parents had built: three bedrooms, one bath, family room, formal living room, kitchen, and two car garage. Grace had insisted that everything in the formal living room was white; the couch, drapes, carpets and all furniture. When guests came over we would all stand at the door and admire the room. No entry was permitted. The family room had sliding glass doors that led to a patio and they were covered by rainbow drapes, the ugliest things I had ever seen in a house, and I can still see them vividly. They got the name because they had every color of the rainbow in them and the colors hung vertically from the rod as if the rainbow lost its direction. Grace had no trouble taking two weeks off when Sheila was born. I could not get to that baby fast enough when she cried. Grace jumped up from wherever she was like a spring. She made the bottles, burped her, changed diapers, picked out all the clothes, and took Sheila to regular doctor's appointments. I was just there thinking perhaps this was normal and she was just being nice since I was so young. I never stepped in or tried to stop her.

Ronnie brought several of his closest friends over to see the baby. After staying just a short time, they would leave to go drinking or shoot pool. What do you call a union between a teenage boy and girl? It's a crush or going steady for a while, but it shouldn't be a marriage. Ronnie and me it was, but we hardly saw each other or wanted to. If he had ever been in love with me, he wasn't any more. If I had ever been in love with, I was too exhausted and confused and just plain young to make a real future with him.

Lacking the driving skills she should have, Mama had never worked up the courage to visit, so Ronnie and I would go there sometimes on the weekends. We took Sheila the first couple of times but then Grace insisted we leave her home so we would have time to ourselves. It was the only time we had fun and got along and it lasted for a few months. We were at Mama's for a weekend and she left to see Grams but hadn't told me how sick Grams had become. Mama called me Friday night to tell me Grams was in a coma and my aunt, uncle and cousins were on their way. She said I should come if I could. Knowing what a disappointment I must have been to Grams, I had not visited her since Sheila was born. I was sure Mama had told her but I was too ashamed to face the woman who loved me unconditionally, fearing I had changed the conditions.

I had arrived at the hospital minutes before her death. Walking the long corridor my heart was pounding and I could feel the tears coming, although I tried hard to choke them back. The halls were quiet and no one else was stirring, except the occasional nurse checking on patients. I pushed open the oversized door and entered the dimly lit room; only a lamp shined slightly in the corner where Mama sat. There was a sanitary smell to the room and there were tubes and machines humming near Grams' bed. The tubes going to the oxygen mask prevented Mama from smoking in the room so she stepped into the hall often to smoke. The family had already gathered outside her room and the doctor was standing by, all of them whispering. I knew things were worse and hated myself for not coming sooner. "Be careful what you say. She's unconscious but might be able to hear you still," the doctor cautioned. She lay on the bed, her long white hair sometimes getting mixed up with the hospital's white sheets. Her eyes were closed but I thought I could see a hint of blue beneath the lids. The soft white skin she had protected from the harshness of the sun her entire life was even paler now, pallid. Her rosy cheeks that had always looked like someone just pinched them were sunken and caved in, blending with the colorless hue of her frail body. She looked so tiny but was always bigger than life to me and all those who knew her. I bent down to her ear and whispered "I love you, Grams! Please don't leave me! Please forgive me. I never meant to hurt you. Please, please!" I couldn't stop sobbing and somewhere a part of me wanted to go with her. Grams' eyes opened briefly as I held her hand and she muttered the words I needed to hear. "I love you." I left the room and went into the empty hallway. Leaning against the wall, my legs gave out from under me and I sank to the floor like a discarded Raggedy Ann doll. In a matter of minutes, everyone, including the doctor, was descending on me to tell me she was gone. My aunt, uncle and cousins all came and took turns hugging me, trying to calm me. My eyes searched for Mama. I saw her standing alone with one tear coming from each eye but she was shaking and smoking, begging the smoke to release her from this moment. When I put my arms around her, she patted me on the back three times and chanted her mantra: "It'll be alright, Carol." My cousins were so kind telling me they knew Grams' loved them but not like she loved me.

The funeral was three days later and the beginning of what I felt would be the end of my life. The one and only person who had been able to hug me when I needed it, tell me when I was wrong, and punish me for it but never stop loving me physically and emotionally, was gone. Mama was so distant that it scared me sometimes but more often frustrated and aggravated me because I couldn't reach her. Ronnie and his family were being nice to me because of the situation. I didn't know what direction my life would take from here and there was no love in sight. Everything was in a rearview mirror now. Daddy left, Grams is gone, and Mama can't love. I had to make the walls thicker, higher, because I knew something bad was always around the corner.

The funeral was held in the little red brick Christian church in Bishop, the church where both Mama and Aunt Roxie were married. We all gathered at the bottom of the steps and everyone was sharing memories. The entire town turned out and after the burial everyone went to Grams' neighbors, Myrtice and Willard's, for a remembrance and feast that would be fit for any holiday. They had lived next door to Grams for their complete married life, probably more than twenty years. My uncle had been assigned to take care of Mama and my aunt was to hold on to me. My cousins gathered around us all. My legs wobbled up the steps with help from Aunt Roxie and at the end of the pews the casket was visible. As my aunt guided me down the aisle, closer and closer to Grams, I could see the glasses on her face and her hair in the bun like always. Her cheeks were rosy again with the aid of her own rouge and I was sure she had on underpants, bra, slip, and one of the many dresses she had picked out over the years for her funeral. Since I had been six, or about the time we moved to Gainesville, Grams had started keeping all of her birthday and Christmas clothes for her funeral. As soon as she opened a box and saw it was clothing she would say "This is so pretty I'm going to save it for my funeral." It became a joke among us all that she had more clothes stashed than what she actually had to wear every day. Gowns and slippers were put away for a nursing home or hospital along with several bras, underwear, and slips. Shoes didn't matter so much. It must have been important to Grams how she looked in death, as much as it did in life.

With Aunt Roxie's help we finally made it to the casket and I saw the Cameo brooch on her dress. It was a must for her to wear anytime she had some fancy event to go to, along with the clip on earrings. Once I commented on how beautiful they were and she laughed and told me it was just costume jewelry but she thought it was pretty, too. I didn't know what the preacher was saying or where Mama was, even if she was right next to me, I was in a complete fog. Closing that casket closed the most important chapters of my life, but I had to go on, for Grams.

Mama went back to Swainsboro, everyone went back to Atlanta and I went back to hell with The Beast. That's how I started to think of her. At first she was kind on the outside but I knew she only wanted me for what I could give her, and that was Sheila. My self esteem was long gone, which gave her even more incentive to be mean. Once again, things went well for a short while during the pity fest. But they only allowed so much time for that before reality took over and The Beast got hungry for my blood again. Two weeks later I was back home with Mama. I wasn't wanted or needed by anyone since Grams left me.

I never thought of taking Sheila. I gave birth to her but she belonged to Grace and I feared The Beast. It wasn't just me who had that unexplainable reaction to her. After all, she couldn't really *do* anything to us. Ronnie and his dad also feared her and we did exactly as she commanded. She ran that house like a military base and she was the drill sergeant. For years I didn't know that Ronnie had a brother who left when he was a teenager because of their mother. I never met his brother or knew what happened, just that he had to get away from her.

James took me back to Swainsboro, back to Mama again, with one bag of clothes. All that I owned. It didn't seem she was very happy to see me but she did ask what had happened as she smoked her cigarettes and made a pot of coffee. She questioned why I didn't bring Sheila and scolded me for leaving her.

"Carol, that's not right. She's your daughter!" I thought maybe she had been told this herself at some point. There was no way to explain that our house was not any better than Ronnie's. Love was absent everywhere.

 She wouldn't understand my fear of Grace. This time the fight only lasted a few days and Ronnie came to get take me back home. I had two homes, one with Mama and one with The Beast. Ronnie missed me and had to have me back. I knew he loved me.

I was greeted at the door by Grace with a sneer saying she was surprised he took me back and I'd better watch it. Her relationship with Sheila was almost merciless as far as I was concerned. If I approached Sheila, Grace would pick her up and only let me hold her for a short while, maybe fearing Sheila would have feelings for me. I had lived with loveless, unemotional people but never with anyone I thought was wicked and cold hearted as I did Grace. She made fun of the clothes I wore, the color of my hair, and soon had Ronnie standing next to her doing the same thing. They would point at me and laugh aloud, making me feel like a clown but in the wrong way. Mama wasn't happy when I was with her so I felt like my home for the present was like the crazy Bates Motel, and Grace was the owner.

Grace did help me out in some ways. For one, she got me a job at the cloth factory where the family worked and with really good pay. Ronnie and I would make enough to get our own place with Sheila and get away from Grace. James tried to stay out of the picture as much as possible so as not to endure the wrath of the woman he lived with. He and Grace shared the same house but that was about all. They never showed affection to each other and slept in separate rooms. James worked the midnight shift and Grace worked four to midnight so they weren't around each other a lot. This bothered neither one of them. James did have far more privileges with Sheila than I did and it was obvious he loved her very much. I worked the same shift as Grace, and she was also my boss. One day I didn't feel well but she demanded that I not miss work because it would look bad for her. Once we got there, she realized how hot I was and sent me to the factory nurse. The nurse took my temperature three times with three different thermometers and each time it read 106 degrees. They called an ambulance and got me to the hospital right away. I had double pneumonia and was very ill. Grace called Mama, who wasn't able to make the trip but asked for daily updates. I was in the hospital for two weeks and Ronnie did not visit me once. James came every day and Grace came when James could watch Sheila. Back home I heard Grace tell Ronnie he should have gone to see me, as sick as I was. He said he was sorry he didn't. He loved me.

I fully recovered after a couple of weeks but things were getting worse at the house and at work. Grace was being down right mean and leaving in the middle of the night while James was at work. She would take Sheila with her and, when I asked what she was doing and where she was going, she told me it was none of my business and not to worry about it. She was just meetin' a friend that she worked with and I was not to mention this to James. For the first time on the way to work one day, I noticed she took a drink from a flask. I was naïve but I knew what a flask was and that it contained alcohol. She started asking me if I wanted to feel better at work, have more energy. Sure, who wouldn't, I thought. I took the first pill she gave me and got the first buzz (other than a cigarette) of my life. Every night at work we took pills and Grace's best friend did too. They would laugh at me, talk about how red my eyes were, and wonder out loud if I would make it through the night.

At work again one night, Grace called me into her office and her best friend was there. They had a favor to ask. Would I call a doctor for them and get a refill on Grace's prescriptions for Darvon, which was an opiate of some sort. I knew the two of them took a lot of it and were trying to get me to do the same. I agreed to call the doctor, not realizing that I would be calling his home at midnight. There was no answering service in those days and it was not unusual to call a doctor at his home, but calling this late at night was unusual. Grace told me to act like I was sick and in pain. With a little persuasion, I was able to get the prescription. It was easy. Now we had to get it filled at the only drugstore in town open all night and it was in the absolute worst part of town for three white women in a Cadillac at one in the morning. I was told to go in and pick up the prescription. I was trembling, afraid I would be shot, beaten, raped or whatever at any minute and was sure that Grace would drive off and leave me there. I was able to get the pills and that's when it hit me. Grace had pulled this same trick many times before, with many different people. Could using the mother of her grandchild be any lower?

Chapter 6

*The Beast and Snookum*

I didn't allow myself to get hooked on the drugs but saw Grace and her friend need more and more. They used me a few more times to get them and then got someone else when they became afraid I'd tell. Everything was coming undone... work, marriage, life in general and Grams was not there to hold me. Ronnie and I never got a place of our own. He wouldn't leave his Mama and she wouldn't allow us to leave and said if we did, we would not get Sheila. Eventually I found a place for myself and made enough money at the factory that I could easily afford to rent it. It was one room in someone's house with only a bed, dresser, and bath. It was perfect for me and I didn't want or need anything other than peace and quiet in my head. My place was about two miles from The Beast, James and Ronnie. I was visiting Sheila one afternoon, which irritated Grace because Sheila was enjoying my company too much for her comfort. She stood and pointed to the door, commanding me with the pointing of her finger and the brutal tone in her voice that I needed to get the hell out of her house and never come back. My eyes were welling with tears, I was alone and afraid, trying desperately to think of anyone who could rescue me, but the list was blank.

All I had were the clothes on my back and a pack of cigarettes, not even a dollar to my name. Grace threatened me that I dare not call a cab but I had no money anyway. I started my walk, crying the entire time, embarrassed for people to see me as I walked on the grassy side of the road. I wondered what they thought had happened as at times I sobbed uncontrollably but just kept walking. First I saw James' car coming towards me and thought he might stop but he just slowed down, looked at me, and kept going. Next came Ronnie speeding by, not even looking at me. I figured Grace had called them home from the pool hall, their usual hangout when they weren't working. I finally made it to my small place, crawled into bed and cried myself to sleep. I didn't go to work because I assumed she had fired me. A few days went by but I never left my room and then one night after midnight in a driving rainstorm, car lights flashed into my windows and woke me up. I thought maybe someone had made the wrong turn. The car horn started to blow so I got up and looked out the window recognizing Grace's Cadillac. I could also see Sheila sitting in the passenger seat in her car seat. I couldn't believe my eyes. She couldn't call me since I had no phone, so she decided to drop by, in a pouring rainstorm after midnight with a baby in the car. Of course she couldn't get out of the car and come to the door; it all had to be on her terms. I softly said a few of my favorite cuss words at the time and went back to bed. She eventually left, as I had hoped.

The next day James showed up and he had always been nice to me despite Grace's discouragement of his efforts. I was so tiny when I was pregnant with Sheila that James started calling me Fatty as a joke. The name stuck our entire relationship. "How come you didn't go out to Grace's car last night, Fatty?" The only answer he got was a cold, hard stare. Grace wanted me home and Sheila was asking for me, he said.

Grace had dared both him and Ronnie to pick me up and if they did, there would be hell to pay. I could hear her screeching demonic beast of a voice in my head. Now it was truly obvious they were both afraid of her but I'm not sure why two grown men were afraid of a five foot six scrawny red headed woman weighing every bit of 110 pounds who stomped through the house like a German soldier. But the fear wasn't physical and never had been. It was all psychological torment. Grace had control over everyone, demeaning, humiliating and conquering everyone in her path, like a fire out of control. She was in command and put the fear of God in everyone she met. I gave in and gave up; going back to the dungeon with James, giving me the opportunity to be with Sheila, but going carefully so as not to awaken The Beast in the house.

Life was good for a few days and even Ronnie treated me with some compassion, although it wasn't long before we were fighting and he threw me against a wall. I had taken a lot of abuse but nothing physical until then. I called Mama crying and she was adamant that I needed to get out before it got worse. James took me back to Mama for what would be the last time. Ronnie would show up on weekends sometimes and there we were again, all hot and bothered just like in the beginning. Mama never knew about any of Ronnie's visits. I left Sheila behind with Grace, feeling it was my only option, having no money and not much will to fight. I knew it was wrong but I was done and had no desire to continue with anything that would involve The Beast. James loved Sheila more than anything or anyone and I knew he would let no harm come to her, not even from that woman. The divorce papers came after Grace did all the necessary paperwork with an attorney. Signing them added another layer to my wall.

I settled in back at home with Mama. She made just enough money to get by so I knew I had to get a job soon. There was a sewing factory in town and that was my place of employment for a short while. I was unable to sew pockets on men's shirts fast enough so they let me go. Yep, not even good enough for a sewin' factory, I told myself. In the meantime, I had started seeing a new boy and it helped get my mind off Ronnie and Sheila. His name was Don and I fell in love again. He was totally opposite from Ronnie, being kind, caring, and loving. Too kind and overly loving. He liked to touch and hug and it made me uncomfortable. I couldn't handle the attention and affection and it allowed me the excuse I needed to push him away. After that, it just became a way of life.

Mama was dating a couple of men at different times. One of them was very handsome and, being a salesman, was only able to see Mama during his short stints in town. The other man lived in town and his name was Snookum Edenfield. Snookum. What kind of a name was that for a man, I asked myself. Mama seemed even more distant than normal and it was evident when we were downtown one night at a little store to get her coffee. I just lollygagged while she shopped and she motioned she was ready to go. We headed for the car and the owner of the store stepped outside and shouted "Ma'am, Ma'am, did you want to pay for that coffee?" The can of coffee was under her arm and I was embarrassed for her as well as myself. I knew she wasn't trying to steal it, she was drifting more than usual and forgot what she was doing.

Snookum was an alcoholic and I could not see what attracted Mama to him unless it was the *I can change him* plague that every woman suffers. Standing about six feet tall, he wasn't bad looking, skinny as a rail, and chain smoked like Mama but instead of coffee he held a glass of hard liquor. He started spending a lot of time at our house so the other man just stopped coming by. I hated this Snookum person and was disgusted when he spent time at the house which was becoming more often. His sister and Mama talked about putting him in a hospital for detoxification and so it was. Mama and I went to visit him and I had never seen anything like it. He was sweating profusely, pale, vomiting, talking to people who weren't even there, and didn't seem to know who we were. I asked Mama what was happening and she said it was just his body trying to rid itself of the alcohol. It was a horrible sight and he went through that for days and was in the hospital for weeks. Was this supposed to make him better, make me approve of him now?

As horrible as it was it took no time before he was drinking again; at our house. I hated him more and Mama didn't seem to mind that I got the car keys from her and spent my nights at Sam's Drive-In when Snookum was at the house. We were deciding what to eat one night and Snookum said we could get the baby out of the freezer. It was the absolute weirdest thing I had ever heard anyone say so I looked at Mama in horror and she told me to pay him no never mind. He was just drunk. He was such a disgusting person to me and that statement just proved it even more. Who would say or even think such a thing? I made a move to get up with intentions of going to the freezer, but Mama waved me off so I sat back down. What a ridiculous statement anyway.

"He's just drunk, Carol."

I wasn't working anywhere and it was summertime. On the Fourth of July a friend asked me to spend the day with her at a motel pool in town. Her relatives owned it so they allowed us to swim as long as we desired. Being about a hundred degrees outside and no sign of a cloud or a breeze, in the water was the place we wanted to be. Summers in southeast Georgia were so hot even the Spanish moss clung closer to the trees seeking relief from the sun. The cement around the pool was scorching hot and you didn't dare get out without stepping on a towel or putting on some flip flops right away. My friend was lucky, being tan and getting tanner, but being the white Irish girl that I was, even after she smeared sunscreen on me all day I still looked like a lobster before the afternoon. Two young girls in bikinis had a lot of cars going by honking their horns, some strangers, some not. Either way we enjoyed the attention and the motel being right on the main drag didn't hurt matters.

I don't know where Mama was during that time and I really didn't care much since she was probably with that Snookum man. I would stay away from home as much as possible and it seemed to work out for both of us. There was no contact with Ronnie, Sheila, or his family and I preferred it that way. I wanted everyone gone just like Edd, J.W., Grams, Ronnie and Sheila. I had no direction, no vision, no obligations, and no desire, but the lust remained. I would meet up with boys I met at Sam's and ride off into the sunset, sometimes sunrise, whenever I wanted.

I loved fast cars and there were plenty around in those days although I didn't have one. I had learned to drive fast from Ronnie and his uncles and with Don, my boyfriend after Ronnie. The first thing noticeable to me anywhere was the car. If it was a fast car, I would flirt until I got to drive it, especially the Chevys with four on the floor. I could lay rubber and shift gears as good as any boy. It was 1967 and my life was filled with boys, fast cars, alcohol, and nobody. But I had a pretty tall wall.

Chapter 7

*An Unquiet Mind*

My behavior was not getting any better, especially with Mama and Snookum being together most of the time and letting me do whatever, whenever I wanted. I wasn't working but Mama never said much about it, so I spent most days at our house alone when I wasn't with friends. I would stay out all night sometimes and come home just in time for Mama to get the car so she could drive to work. I was eighteen and she didn't say much to me, just kept to herself. The only time I needed money was to buy cigarettes and at fifty cents a pack it wasn't hard. It was couch change.

Then the day came on Monday, August 7, 1967, that set the course for the rest of our lives. While searching for something to eat, I opened the big white upright freezer, the one J.W. had bought for Mama years ago. It sat in the dining room of our tiny house and looked so out of place next to the cherry wood dining table and chairs with the silk padded seats. I opened the big door and saw nothing to eat but something looked out of place. It was a towel with big green and white stripes, just like the ones in the linen closet. The baby lay there, cuddled like it was in a blanket trying to stay warm.

"Mama, Mama come home quick!" I hardly had the breath to speak. The two women I had dragged to the house were in shock, all the while getting the police on the neighbor's phone.

"What's the matter now, Carol?"

"There's a baby in the freeza, Mama! There's a baby in the freeza!" The line went dead and I knew she was hurrying home. Coming home to comfort me and talk to the police to find out what happened. Who had stolen their way into our house and done such a hideous thing? Our house was never locked but no one else locked their doors either. Oh Lord my mind was spinnin' and my stomach was in my throat.

Mama would be home soon to ease my ramblin' mind as I was quickly falling apart. My legs felt like rubber, surely to collapse any time. My body was numb and I didn't know how I was still breathing. I was cold, hot, sweaty, clammy, shivering, and anesthetized all at the same time.

Soon the police were everywhere; in the house, the yard, our lives. The Georgia Bureau of Investigation came soon after the local police. I was still shaking, wondering if my breath was leaving me for good and maybe I was going to die. I had to hold out until Mama arrived. The police had the two neighbor women off to the side, talking to them quietly. Two men from the Georgia Bureau of Investigation took me to a chair and tried to calm me, asking where Mama was. I noticed they were wearing suits and not uniforms like Sheriff Josh or his deputy, Shot Strange. I couldn't look at their faces or anyone else's. She was on her way home, I told them. They wanted to ask me some questions so I nodded my head that they could.

"Now Ms. Carol, what made you open that freeza today?"

"Have you been by yourself all day"?

"What was the first thing you did, Ms. Carol, afta you opened the freeza"?

"Who all lives in this house 'sides you and yor mama?"

"Why didn't you just call the police instead of runnin' to Ms. Marjorie's"?

"Why did you call your mama first?"

I heard the sound of Mama's Dodge in front of the house. With police cars all around, I'm sure she didn't know where to park. Simple things like that confused Mama sometimes. She came through the front door and into the crowd in the small living room.

"Afternoon, Ms. Jessie. We have a bad situation here." said Sheriff Josh. "Me and Shot need to talk to you, Ms. Jessie."

 In a small town, everybody knew everybody and if you didn't actually know them, you knew someone who did. Mama had known Sheriff Josh and also Deputy Shot Strange for years and vice versa. Mama pushed past Sheriff Josh during his attempt at asking questions and headed straight towards the bathroom, which was more in my direction. She was coming to comfort me, I thought. But no, she didn't stop even when I cried out to her.

"Mama, what's happened?"

She entered the bathroom and closed the door while the GBI and local police hovered nearby, waiting for her to come out. The door soon opened and Mama was nervously lighting a cigarette. She was going through almost the same questions I had endured and like me she had no answers. Why had someone done this to us? Mama said she just had no idea how that baby coulda got in the freeza.

"A baby? My Gawd!" Mama had no other words.

Without even me noticing, some of my other friends had shown up after they heard all the rigmarole at our house. The GBI suggested it might be a good idea for me to get out of the house for a while and catch my breath, try to calm myself. Mama would stay at the house with the police until all the evidence was taken care of. That was a nice way of putting it, I guess.

While at my friend's house, the same two GBI agents came over and asked to speak with me. We sat in the living room with my friend sitting next to me for support. They said they stopped by to check on me, to see if I was ok, and only stayed for a couple of minutes. As we all stood for them to leave, Investigator Kettle put his arm on my shoulder and said he was sorry but someone was gonna have to be arrested for murder and it might be someone I was close to. At that moment my heart stopped when I looked in his eyes with confusion wondering who he was talking about. Again I wondered who had come into our house and done such an unspeakable thing.

My friend took me back to Mama's as I was worried about what was going on there. Everyone had gone. No police cars lined the streets and the neighbors were no longer gawking. Walking towards the front door I could see Mama through the screen, sitting in the rocker with a cup of coffee and a cigarette. Georgia in August and it was near a hundred degrees but Mama needed her coffee. As much as I wanted answers, I knew Mama couldn't give them to me and she sat and stared straight ahead as if I wasn't there. Looking from the corner of my eye, I could see the freezer was still there. Was the baby there, too? The mere thought of such a thing made me want to throw up. They left that horrible white coffin in our house still running like it had a normal purpose. I went to my room and prayed to Jesus that this would end as a nightmare and when I woke up life would be just as it had been. I sobbed harder than I ever had in my short life, at times not being able to catch my breath. I was never going to be able to stop. Sometimes you think your life is bad until something even worse happens.

All this time I had not even thought about Ronnie but the next thing I knew, his arms were around my shoulders coaxing me to stop crying.

"Get some shit together, we're leaving."

I had no mind of my own and was incapable of making a decision so I did as I was told. Later I found out that a friend had called Ronnie and told him what had happened. She said that at first he didn't believe her and thought it was one of my pathetic attempts to get him back, but soon realized it was true. Ronnie helped me throw some clothes into a bag and I stopped next to Mama, still sitting in the rocker moving' slowly to and fro, like she used to do on Grams' porch swing. I put my arms around her while I was down on my knees sobbing uncontrollably again, hoping that just this once she could put her arms around me. I asked if I should go with Ronnie, realizing now she would be left alone. But Mama had already been alone for a long time.

"It'll be alright," she said and patted me on the back. There were no tears coming from her eyes but maybe she had cried while I was gone.

We got to Ronnie's car and he told me he had made the hour and a half drive in just over an hour, driving faster than he ever had. Ronnie said he had opened the screen door to the house and just walked in as usual. Mama looked up at him and said "Carol got me in trouble today." He demanded to know where I was and then saw me in my room. The trip back to Milledgeville was solemn and sober. Not much transpired between us and there was no room in my brain for words of any kind since it was filled with pictures. Pictures of a freeza' door open wide with a green and white towel. Pictures of a doll wrapped up in the towel. Oh no, it wasn't a doll, they said. Sobbing, sobbing, and sobbing. Would I ever be able to stop, I asked myself again.

"You alright, Fatty?" James asked as we entered the house.

I couldn't answer but looked at Grace at she guided me to my room with a hand gesture. The three of them stood outside the bedroom whispering, asking Ronnie what the hell happened. It is bad when people whisper. I heard Grace say they should keep an eye on me since I might do something stupid, like try to kill myself. That would have taken much more energy than I had and would also require thinking. I was incapable of either act.

I slept for hours and when I woke, James told me I needed to call my aunt and uncle in Atlanta. I hadn't thought of that or anything that I should do. James stayed at the phone while I called. My cousin Cid answered, the only boy of the four siblings and the oldest. Uncle Austin was out of town on business and Aunt Roxie was in Ohio going to school for her Master's and staying with friends. Somehow the words came out that I had found a baby in the freezer of our house. It sounded like nonsense and at that point James took the phone. He explained what had happened and told the kids to get Uncle Austin directly.

Cid was able to get Uncle Austin and asked when he was coming home. He answered he would leave after dinner but Cid told him he needed to leave immediately and then he told him why. Uncle Austin told Cid not to tell my aunt.

The phone rang soon and James answered. I could tell by his quiet voice that it was my uncle and James was doing his best to describe the events of the day. The conversation ended quickly and James said my uncle would soon be on his way to Swainsboro to see Mama. Another call came almost immediately after and it was Sheriff Josh telling James that Mama had been arrested for murder. Mama had given the sheriff the phone number and asked him to call me. Sheriff Josh was a good sheriff but also a good man and never once treated any of us badly. As rough as his job was, he was able to carry out his duties with grace and compassion.

Mama was in jail. My head was spinning again and my life was spinning out of control. What was I supposed to do? There had to be something I needed to do but I was eighteen and didn't know about this part of life. James took over and did my thinking for me. He notified my uncle that when he got to Swainsboro, Mama would be in jail.

Uncle Austin made it to Swainsboro the next day and went directly to the jail, saying he was there to see Ms. Jessie. Not knowing my uncle, Sherriff Josh asked him what he had to do with any of this. Uncle Austin introduced himself as Mama's brother-in-law and was led upstairs to Mama's cell. There was a woman with her and she was familiar to my uncle. He had seen her before on visits to our house, even as far back as when Mama and J.W. were married. Just like most people in town, he only knew her as Ma since that was the only way she was ever addressed. Ma was different than the other women in town. She wore flannel shirts, cuffed jeans, and no makeup. She hunted and fished and could drink any man under the table. The sheriff had let Ma stay as long as she wanted and it would be the same for anyone who came to see Mama. The little red brick jail had only room downstairs for three cells, and the couple who made the food for the inmates lived upstairs. There was one cell up there and it was Mama's. There had never been a woman in there before but there was a separate room just in case the jail got overfilled. Uncle Austin tried to talk to Mama but she told him the same as everyone... that she just had no idea how all of it had happened. He knew it was futile to go on so he told her he would get a lawyer and she said get Mr. John B. Spivey.

Uncle Austin tried to hide the situation from his wife of almost twenty years for a short time but the news was too big. As my aunt's friends were watching the ten minute news at six o'clock in Ohio, they saw the story of a baby found frozen in the home of a Ms. Jessie Cobb. They recognized the name and went straight to my aunt who was in another room.

"You must be mistaken" my aunt said. "That just can't be my sista."

She called home, talked to Cid, and found out the truth. Even though he had been told by his daddy not to tell, Aunt Roxie already knew when she called. Cid told his mama that his daddy had already left to see her sister. It was true. She left Ohio immediately to fly home and be with Ms. Jessie.

The next day James took me to Swainsboro to meet with my uncle. I still had no answers for him and didn't know any more than I did the day before. We all went to the jail and Uncle Austin told Deputy Strange we all wanted to see Ms. Jessie. We walked up the stairs and I was surprised at how big the room, or cell, was. The walls were painted grey and very. There was a cot against a wall and two windows, one on each outside wall, since the room was on a corner. The bars on the windows were a solemn reminder that this was no ordinary room. It was a jail cell, Mama's cell. Unlike the other cells for the men, Mama's had a separate room with a bathroom included in the cell. I walked in and saw writing on the wall above the sink that had been done with red lipstick. The words were *God help me*. I sat down next to Mama and calmly asked if she had written them. She said no, the words were already there, but I didn't believe her. Uncle

Austin made Mama aware that he had already met with Mr. Spivey and he and his partner, Mr. Carlton, were takin' her case. It would be very expensive and my uncle asked if Mama had any money at all. She said no and there was nothing of worth to sell since we rented the house. Aunt Roxie and Uncle Austin would have to come up with the money if they wanted to help Mama, and they did. We stayed for an hour or so and left so Mama could eat lunch. Meals were prepared in the jail and as good as any you could get in town. Everything was homemade and fresh with lots of vegetables, which Mama loved. It was usual for her to have barbeque, Brunswick stew, cornbread, fish, hush puppies, turnip greens, fried okra, and sweet tea and of course Mama was allowed all the coffee she wanted. She filled the ash tray in her cell by the hour so she needed a garbage can. Mama was always able to withdraw from any situation and now she needed all of her skills to be someplace other than the Swainsboro jail.

James, with my uncle and me, went a few blocks from the jail for lunch. There were stares and whispers and I didn't want to know what they were saying. It was an odd out of place feeling that I had dealt with before when I left Grams. The townsfolk knew who I was but I was being escorted by two out-of-towners, which provided even more fodder. Being me now was excruciating and Mama was being tried right there, right then, in that little eatery. The gossip and speculation started the first day, as usual.

We cut our lunch short and headed back to see Mama before we all left town. Leaving Mama left me numb. I saw her behind the bars, cigarette in hand saying "Bye, bye, it'll be alright." I left my child behind before this and now I had left Mama, alone, with no one. Sobbing uncontrollably was common for me and it happened every day for so many days, it was impossible to take inventory. Feeling worthless, alone and totally insignificant in the scheme of life, I trekked back to Milledgeville with James and Uncle Austin went back to Atlanta to comfort Aunt Roxie.

James and I were quiet on the way back and my own thoughts scared me so much that I didn't allow myself to say them out loud. Replaying the event in my head over and over, I would recall what Snookum had said just weeks ago about a baby in the freezer. He knew! The son of a bitch was the father. No, my Mama would never agree to something so heinous. But then where did the baby come from? Mama had not been pregnant. Was it me? Did I do it? No, I had only been pregnant once, with Sheila. Who would have had a baby and put it in a freezer, in our house? What did Snookum have to do with it? I knew in my heart and intellectually it had to be something. Next week we were meeting with Mr. Spivey and I would tell him about Snookum. Wait, what was I thinking? Mama was in jail for something she had nothing to do with unless that man made her defy her own will. This was not happening to me, to Mama. I was having that bad dream again and just needed to wake up. I looked over at James with the big cigar in his mouth concentrating on keeping the big Caddy on the country roads, but I knew he was thinking about it, too.

## Chapter 8

*Changing Homes, Again*

We arrived back in Milledgeville with Ronnie and Grace waiting at the house. Once again I went straight to the bedroom and my tears kept flowing like a raging river that couldn't be damned. Ronnie came in trying to comfort me but it was no use. I was in another world, a world of horror and unforgiving nightmares that would never end. With every turn of my head I saw a baby, that baby, looking like a doll hidden in a place for a sadistic game of some sort; one that Snookum had devised during his many drunken, indistinct days.

"Are you alright?" they kept asking me.

"NO, I WILL NEVER BE ALRIGHT!" The walls were not thick enough, high enough or as strong as they should be.

That's what screamed in my head but only in my head as I feared that saying it out loud would make it true. I spent the next few days in bed until the weekend came and Ronnie took me to see Mama in jail. We sat and talked as if nothing had happened and life just went on as usual; Mama smoking one cigarette after another with her free hand holding her coffee. The usual. Going back to Swainsboro brought rumors to the forefront that I didn't want to know about but couldn't help but overhear at lunch or at the store when we bought smokes or gas. The whispers and looks were no surprise but oddly enough to me, Ronnie did all he could to protect me. The local gossip included the idea that Mama had buried many babies in the yard and they (there was always a "they") would eventually dig up the yard to look for remains. This became my second introduction to the cruelty that comes so easy to people. My first had been meeting Grace, aka The Beast.

Ronnie took me on weekends several times to see Mama. My Aunt Roxie and Uncle Austin arranged to meet me and James at the house in Swainsboro. Driving up to the house for the first time since that day, I felt sick at my stomach and wondered what remained. Was the freezer still there? The furniture? The house looked the same, as if nothing had happened, and the neighbors were all either at work or hiding. None of the yard was dug up, as the nasty rumors had said it had been. James and I arrived first and walked to the screen door, pulling it open to gain entry through the wooden front door, which was unlocked as always. My eyes went to the rocking chair that Mama and I shared and then to the left where the TV, couch and end tables sat. The end table between the rocking chair and the couch was the one that held the ashtray and it was there, filled with cigarettes as if Mama had just stepped out for a walk. I knew I had to look to the right now, toward the dining area where the big white coffin stood. I held my breath and heard James ask, "Are you alright, Fatty?" From the corner of my eye, the white color was illuminating; shining as if a spotlight was focused directly on it. It was still there. Was the baby there, too? I didn't want to open the door and wouldn't. Nor would I even walk in that direction.

I heard my aunt's voice and the next thing I knew her arms were fully around me, holding me tight like Grams would have.

"We're gonna get through this, honey," she said.

The floodgates opened and I felt myself almost collapse in her arms as I sobbed my uncontrollable river of tears. She held onto me in a way that I knew she wouldn't let me go and for a moment, I was safe. After gaining my composure, I held hands with my aunt as we, along with James and my uncle, walked the few steps to Mama's bedroom. The bed was in the middle of the small room with a dresser to the left. Mama had not had this bedroom suite too long and it was made of a beautiful mahogany. The bed was bare of sheets and the mattress, a monster in itself, stood out calling *look at me, look at me*! There was a big stain in the middle, maybe two feet wide in an odd shape, an abstract. Aunt Roxie's first comment was that it was probably a stain from childbirth. The speculation started now between my aunt and uncle that perhaps Snookum had given

Mama somethin' to knock her out during the delivery, otherwise, why didn't I hear screams of childbirth? Was I even there, they wondered, or maybe he drugged me, too. Either way, I never knew of Mama having a baby because I didn't know she was pregnant and didn't believe she ever was. For the first time it was brought up that maybe someone else had been with Mama, someone who helped with delivery. That someone had to be Ma. She was the only friend close to Mama and also one who could handle any situation, including cleaning her own game. Aunt Roxie found it hard to believe that Snookum and Mama could have pulled this off by themselves and it made me wonder. But not for long, as I reminded myself that my Mama would never be able to do anything of the kind and even though she was distant and cold, she was kind and caring to everyone; just at a safe distance.

The talks began of what to do with the furniture and An Unquiet Mind. The furniture items were doled out to family members in Athens and Ronnie's dad James agreed to take and dispose of the freezer. That was the last time I entered or saw that house until forty years later.

It was decided for me that I would stay with my aunt and uncle in Atlanta. They both knew how much I hated staying with The Beast and, since Ronnie and I were divorced, it seemed the right thing to do. I went back home with James and said my goodbyes to Sheila and Ronnie and gladly to The Beast. James soon took me to Atlanta and my cousins were waiting for me with hugs and sympathy like any brothers or sisters would be. The house was enormous, even by Atlanta standards ,with the downstairs consisting of a formal dining room, formal living room, big kitchen with two steps down to a family room and then a rumpus room,  which was big enough to hold maybe fifty people, with a bathroom off to the side. Upstairs were five bedrooms, with the master having a full bath and then another in the hall. I would bunk with Suzanne, who was closest to my age except for Cid. The house sat on the top of a big hill on a cul-de-sac and one of the Atlanta Falcons coaches lived next door. My uncle had obviously done well for his family, being a salesman for a national company. He was a handsome man and quite the flirt, which enabled him to do his job even better. He smoked a pipe most of the time and always had a joke to tell, constantly smiling except when yelling at the four kids—five, with me—causing havoc throughout the house. Aunt Roxie was a beautiful woman with Irish red hair and skin like milk. The two of them made a striking couple and their children were a credit to their genes. It was tense at first, everyone afraid they would say the wrong thing or upset me, but that soon gave way to laughs at the dinner table, making me feel at home. It was obvious no one wanted to pressure me or ask too much but every night Suzanne and I talked and, a little at a time, I began telling her my feelings. How I thought I might go crazy, that Mama had never been able to care for me or show me love. It was hard for her to understand since their family was so opposite, lovin' and huggin' all the time. We chalked some of it up to me being an only child and the rest to, well, we didn't know what it was.

Aunt Roxie tried to talk about Mama without upsetting me. She wanted me to know Mama was sick and none of it was my fault. She was nervous at times when we sat down for our chats but once she told me something she thought I should know. "When your Grams was dying, she said to me, take care of Jessie. Honey she knew something was wrong with Jessie and she had always known. She knew you were strong and would be alright. You are strong and you have to go on, for your Grams."

September came and Mama was being sent to Central State Hospital in Milledgeville, Georgia, for a psychiatric evaluation, part of the court process. Mr. Spivey had ordered an evaluation of Mama's sanity, thinking it could help her case. Being only eighteen I didn't know much about CSH or mental illness. Letters started arriving from the hospital with Mama's diagnosis. They contained words like "paranoid schizophrenia" and "psychosis." Big words I had never heard of but I knew it meant something was wrong with Mama and it sounded serious. Aunt Roxie did her best to explain and even tried to comfort me by saying that Mama was very sick and not responsible for what had happened. Some of it didn't matter since I knew she didn't do anything but now I was wondering why I didn't know she was sick. It is a sickness you can't see, my aunt would explain.

Mama stayed at CSH for two months and was seen by nine doctors at one time and five at another. Dr. Mendoza was her assigned psychiatrist but she saw many other doctors for medications and stabilization. They will fix her, I thought, just like they fix a broken arm, and she will be fine. We weren't able to visit her during her stay at the hospital so it was December before we went back to Swainsboro. It was a three-hour trip just to get there. My aunt and uncle had been communicating by phone and mail with Mama's attorneys but we would see them in person on our next trip. I had to tell the attorneys what Snookum had said about the baby in the freezer and this would all be taken care of finally, I thought.

On the one hand, this was the worst time of my life. On the other hand, I really enjoyed my time with my cousins and saw what a real family looked like and, more importantly, acted like. They were all in school and I stayed home during the day, assuming I was awaiting Mama's fate to determine the rest of my life. Aunt Roxie did mention my getting back into school but not until "afta." Christmas came while I was still with them and I was unexpectedly showered with gifts from clothes to jewelry. The kids had decided to have a plaque made for their Mama and daddy with "World's Best Family" on it. They asked me what I thought and I told them it was something unique and I wouldn't have thought of it myself.

On Christmas day we all gathered in the rumpus room around the eight-foot Douglas fir tree. It was by far the biggest tree I had ever seen in a house and it was real. We had all gone with Uncle Austin to pick it up and bring it home on top of the station wagon. It was time for my aunt and uncle to open their special gift and the smile on their faces was priceless to me. My aunt had a tear in her eye, reading to herself that she was part of the best family in the world. The plaque was passed around to all of us and I saw it for the first time. It was beautiful red wood with the engravings in gold. I passed it to my cousin Lisa.

C. Saxon An Unquiet Mind

"Did you look at it?" she asked, handing it back to me.

I looked again and to my amazement, the family names were all listed: first my aunt and uncle, then Cid, Suzanne, Lisa, Melanie........and Carol. I took a deep breath and was covered in bodies and arms, hugs and kisses and "We love you's." I remembered Grams and her love for me. Love I had been denied for so long but I didn't even know how much I missed it or needed it. My new family had embraced me in every aspect of the word and my heart was full with pride and adoration.

Chapter 9

*Small Town Justice*

We received word that Mama was going back to Swainsboro at the end of November and return to her cell. The doctor's diagnosis had been sent to her lawyers and the prosecutor. With my aunt and uncle, we hurried down to see her and met with Mr. Spivey and Mr. Carlton. Not pretending to understand anything of what was going to happen, we were told it was good that Mama was sick and that would be her defense. The trial would be held on January 9, 1968. A little over a month from now, Mama would be on trial for her life. Arrested in August and tried five months later. Justice worked faster back then.

I was shy and stayed in the background as much as possible, begging for anonymity with all that had happened in the past. As everyone was discussing the trial, I blurted out what Snookum had said that day about the baby being in the freeza' at our house. Mr. Spivey said that even though he found it interesting it was hearsay and would not be allowed in court. Furthermore, I was going to be a witness for the prosecution and testify against my mama. Confounded. That's what described me at that very moment. I loved my mama so how did they expect me to say bad things? Mr. Spivey assured me that it was all just legalities and I was not to worry 'bout it. The people testifyin' would be sequestered in a room togetha, he told me, so no one would be able to talk about my mama. Lord God Almighty. What in the world was this all gonna be like?

We all headed up to see Mama and got there just in time for her lunch. She seemed to enjoy the food, as any true southerner would. Today she was having pecan pie for dessert and my mouth watered. We discussed what we were told about the trial, which was met with um hums and alrights from Mama. Asked about her trip to CSH, she said everyone was real nice but they thought she was crazy. My aunt mumbled something about the crazier the betta' at this point. We told Mama we would be back around Christmas and, when we did return, we had a bag full of cartons of cigarettes that Uncle Austin had picked up for her. It was the same thing we always took but this time there was a red bow around the bag. Mama acted like it was a necklace of pure gold.

After getting back home to Atlanta, my aunt tried to prepare me for the trial. She told me what kind of questions they would ask and that the prosecutor would try to make me say bad things about Mama. She mentioned it was a good thing I would be sequestered and would not be able to hear all the testimony. I wasn't sure what she meant exactly.

My Aunt Sissy, who was not a real aunt and I'm really not sure how she was related, lived not too far away in Watkinsville and visited a couple of times. She worked in the school system as a visiting teacher back then, making sure no kids were being abused, especially the black children. I had seen her lots of times as I was growing up and was very fond of her. Between my Aunt Roxie and her, it was decided that after Mama's trial, I would get therapy myself in a hospital, but not CSH. Central State Hospital was for schizophrenics, manic-depressives, criminals and the insane. They didn't think I belonged in a place like that but why was Mama there, I wondered. And why did they think I needed to be in a hospital at all? Yes, something horrible had happened but it would all be alright. Mama said so. I wasn't looking forward to leaving the family but they had been so kind to me that I thought they knew best. Besides, I sure had made no plans for myself yet.

Time flew after the holidays and it was January 9 before we knew it. Aunt Roxie bought Mama a plain black dress for the trial and we all wore our Sunday best. When you're going to court, you wear your Sunday best so that people will look at you as being normal, just like them. We met Mr. Spivey and Mr. Carlton at the courthouse and briefly went over what was going to happen. The first order of business was jury selection, which started at 10:00 a.m. Four panels of twelve jurors each were examined and asked their feelings on capital punishment, and whether they had biases or prejudices. At 11:05 a.m., twelve jurors were seated, after the defense had struck thirteen. I was allowed to be present for the selection of the jury, and then was whisked away to a room to be sequestered with the others. The *Swainsboro Forest Blade* would later describe the jury as "10 white men, a Negro man and a Negro woman." There I was in a room with fifteen people who would testify against my mama. Then I saw him. Snookum. We had to spend our time in the same small room. He looked away when I glanced at him, like any coward would. I had seen him only once after *that day* and only for a brief time at Mr. Spivey's office. When we were alone for a minute he asked me why I had to do what I did. After giving him a look of inquiry, he clarified by asking directly why I had to call the police.

"Why did you have to do that to yor mama, Carol? We could have handled it and you never needed to call the police. Look what you've done," he said.

I had done some bad things, crazy things, but I knew what was right and wrong. My disgust for him nearly choked me and I tasted regurgitation in my mouth. Once again, I told Mr. Spivey about the conversation, but it meant nothing. The bastard should rot in hell. The rest of the witnesses were all real careful about how they spoke and I was sure if I hadn't been there, the conversation would have been much different. In a small southern town where everybody knows everybody there's not much to talk about that everyone doesn't already know. Everyone was cordial to each other but I was as nervous as a long tailed cat in a room full of rockin' chairs.

I was the second witness called. The door opened and I was escorted by the bailiff to the stand where I was sworn in. Mama sat nearby in her black dress, her head down while she chewed on her thumbnail. Mr. Spivey winked at me as if telling me it would be alright and not to worry. I was shaking, visibly, and then I saw what my eyes had trouble believing. In the courtroom balcony stood my history teacher with the kids I had grown up with. What on earth was going on? A field trip to watch a fellow student testify at her mother's trial? Or were they just there to witness small town justice? It was devastating and my mind wanted to shut down and I wanted to become invisible or just get up and run away. But then I heard a noise and realized it was the prosecutor asking me a question. I told myself to think, not about the three hundred or so people, but about saving Mama. I testified under oath that I did not know Mama was ever pregnant, that it was not unusual for her to gain and lose weight during the year, and that the house was never locked. Also I stated that Mama had changed over the past year and did not seem to care how she looked or about taking care of herself. I was asked where I was on the certain dates involved and exactly how the events unfolded for me on that August day. After being dismissed I looked up to the balcony one more time, knowing another nightmare had been added to my ever-growing list. The wall needed to be higher still.

Once one witness was back in the witness room, the next was called and those of remaining behind awaited their return, stifling in a room full of tension from heat and circumstance. Soon they were calling Snookum, and I hoped he died in the courtroom. Instead he returned after a brief period. He had been coached by Mama's lawyers and testified that he was a frequent visitor to the house and had seen changes in Mama over the last year, includin' her not carin' so much about how she looked. He knew nothin' about her bein' pregnant, of course. He couldn't look at me but I stared at him, hoping to catch his eye so he could see the hate in mine. Coward. Almost everyone Mama worked with at the Ford place was called as a witness. They all said much of the same thing; that Mama had gained weight and looked her heaviest around the Fourth of July, the time the baby was supposedly put in the freezer. Most of the men said they thought she might be pregnant, but no one ever asked and it was never brought up. They all said she looked smaller after the Fourth of July. I was there. Why didn't I notice any of this? How could these friends of Mama's be talking like this?

Deputy Shot Strange said when he informed Mama of her rights, while still at the house, she had denied any knowledge of a child. About two hours late, he testified, Mama told him she remembered the pregnancy and going into labor. Mama told the deputy and the GBI agent that she blacked out and had no idea what had happened until the baby was found at her house. This brought about an argument between the state and Mr. Spivey on whether Mama's statement was an admission of guilt or a confession. The jury was dismissed and the judge ruled it as an admission and instructed them to proceed using that term when they examined the deputy. The difference between the two is that an admission does not accept personal responsibility for the crime, the judge said. Mama told Deputy Strange that she had never been to a doctor or taken any medications during the pregnancy. I was recalled for more testimony about the towel (were there others like it in our house) and about Mama's changing moods.

Being sequestered for the trial, I didn't know any of the testimony until my aunt explained some of it. She hid the Swainsboro paper from me and thought it wouldn't be healthy for me to read the details. Forty years later, with the help of my dear friend still living in Swainsboro, I was able to get a copy and read all of the following details.

Dr. Moye, the county physician, told the court he performed an autopsy on the baby the day after it was discovered. He said the child was female and, although through his examination of the lungs he determined she had been alive, it was impossible to determine if she was alive when placed in the freezer. She weighed 7 pounds, 15 ounces and was a full term baby. Cause of death was strangulation. There were bruise marks on both sides of the throat, more on the right side, but what caused the marks was undeterminable. Even after forty years passed before I read this information, I was still shocked to the core. I hated that man, Snookum, all over again and hoped by now he was rotting in hell.

Mr. Sullinger was the toxicologist with the state crime lab and had assisted with the autopsy. He told the court that he agreed with Dr. Moye that the baby had died of strangulation but evidence also pointed to the bruise marks having been achieved by someone using their hands. He further stated the child's blood had not developed enough to match it with Mama's type O blood.

Mama's lawyers only had three witnesses since Mama never took the stand. The three were all staff doctors at Central State Hospital in Milledgeville; Dr. Craig was superintendant, Dr. Mendoza was director of the unit where Mama stayed after her evaluation, and Dr. Stences was director of maximum security, where inmates like Mama were held for observation.  Dr. Craig's testimony held the most weight since he was the director. He stated that Mama had seen fifteen doctors when she was there for two months and the diagnosis was conclusive: schizophrenia with paranoid tendencies. He testified she probably had this for years or most of her life but it was not uncommon for her to function in a daily routine. When asked if she could have fooled the doctors, he replied that some had tried but it was highly unlikely. It was a Catch 22. No one wants their Mama to be mentally ill, but being true or not didn't matter if it would save her.

The judge ordered everyone to lunch and the other witnesses were allowed to eat at the café across the street. Mr. Spivey had food brought in for the family at his office so we could go over the trial. He felt things were going our way after testimony from the doctors confirmed Mama's sickness. What sickness? How could all of this still be happening? When was I going to wake up?

Court resumed with more of the same and wrapped up at 4:54 p.m. with short arguments by counsel. Mama's defense team argued that all evidence was circumstantial and that a plea of not guilty should be returned. The state countered that there was evidence Mama had been pregnant and that the child had been killed by someone's hands while being strangled, and since Mama didn't seek medical attention, she was guilty of murder by neglect. Yet it takes two to make a baby. No questions were ever brought up about who the father was or what role he may have played in planning the events. Why? No one was ever interested in the truth.

We were all released for supper and the jury was to start deliberations immediately after that one hour break. My good friend Daphne and her mother invited me to their house for a sandwich and tea and the lawyers, along with my family, thought it would be a good idea for me to get away from everything for a little while. Daphne and I sat at the table while her mother fiddled nervously around the kitchen. As with most people I had been around lately, she was fearful that she might say something wrong so she just mentioned casually that she knew I must be tired after such a tryin' day. Their kindness has never been forgotten. Everyone speculated that the jury would probably want to retire and we would get the verdict in the morning. The phone rang a little after eight o'clock that same night and we were told to get to the courthouse quick. Ms. Parrish took us back and we walked in to about a hundred people in the courtroom, fewer than there had been all day. The jury had come back after only one hour and five minutes. The trial had started at ten that same morning to pick a jury. Testimony started a little after eleven, with a break for lunch and supper. It was now a little after nine at night and Mama sat at the defense table, book-ended by her lawyers and with us directly behind her. My aunt was holding on to me and my uncle was holding on to my aunt. Mama and all were asked to rise for the reading of the verdict by the court clerk and we all held our breath. It was the longest pause of my life.

"Not guilty by reason of insanity."

Mama cried, not out loud, but softly as if not to disturb anyone. The smaller crowd in the courtroom collectively sighed, most as if in relief. So many people knew Mama since she worked at the Ford place for eight years and she was respected for her work ethic and professionalism. This entire fiasco shocked the little town and residents were in disbelief that this could have ever happened. But it did and now Mama would be the only one suffering the consequences, even though it took two to make that baby. By being found "insane," she would serve a minimum of one year at Central State Hospital and be released only when the hospital felt she was "cured." Aunt Roxie and I trembled in unison, both reaching out for Mama as soon as the verdict was read.

"Thank Gawd" my aunt muttered as she wept. Mama looked our way and said, "It'll be alright."

It wasn't going to be alright. It never had been and never would be. There would be a ripple effect from my mama's problems into my own life, giving us more in common than I could have imagined.

Chapter 10

*The Hospitals*

"We can't let her be alone in that police car with that man, just him and her for that long ride." My Aunt Roxie was worried. She was talking about Mama and the ride to Central State Hospital in Milledgeville, Georgia. Mama was on her way to serve the sentence that was handed down just a mere twelve hours before.

Driving down that winding Georgia country road with my Aunt Roxie and Uncle Austin, all I could do was sit in the backseat and stare ahead at the police car in front of us. Mama was sitting in the front seat with the officer, flicking one cigarette filter after another out the window of the car. My aunt and uncle tried to carry on a quiet conversation in the front seat, probably hoping I wasn't listening or at least not paying too much attention to what they were saying. They talked quietly about the horrors of the place Mama was going. It wasn't just any hospital. Central State Hospital was the largest insane asylum in the United States.

While the car bounced gently over the road, I sat there hoping someone would shake me and tell me to wake up, tell me this had all been a bad dream, a nightmare. How could this be happening? How could I have ever imagined this day or the days that sat down before this one and dared us to live without memories. It was certainly not something I had ever imagined possible in all my life. My mama, anxious at times, saddened at others, had trouble making emotional ties with anyone. She wasn't a killer, a murderer, but this short trial in Georgia condemned us both to torture forever.

Then we were there, at the threshold of hell with Mama just ahead of us. As we turned onto the property we were greeted by huge magnolia trees lining both sides of the long driveway, protected from the sun by live oaks. The building was a big, white, four-story brick building, four columns rising to the third floor. There was even a dome on top made of copper. It looked like it could have been an old Georgia mansion where rich white people could sit on the porch in rockin' chairs drinking mint juleps. The beautifully tended grounds disguised the reality of the residents remanded there. The breathtaking scenery should have put me at ease but instead made my stomach churn.

Both cars pulled up front to the mansion and parked. Once out of our cars, we walked up the steps together with Mama and the police officer rang the bell. A woman sitting at a desk could see us through the big windows in the doors. She greeted us like visitors, politely and curtly, asking the officer if my Mama was Ms. Jessie. Indeed.

The waiting room was large with chairs and a couch, but it smelled like stale smoke and musty wet carpet. This was not how I had imagined a Georgia mansion would smell. I thought to myself that the carpet smelled like it needed a proper airin'.

The room was drab despite the bright red accent pieces meant to offset the horrible reality. The interior walls of this faux mansion were painted an off-white color with paintings hung all around. They were mostly of men on horseback, again an ode to a southern plantation, I was sure.

As I stood there numb and scared, the officer went about the business of getting Mama settled. He handed the woman some paperwork as she sat back down at the desk. She announced in that same politely curt voice that a nurse would be with us directly.

None of us knew what to do, to say, or how to act. Mama was no help; she just stood there shifting, fidgeting, moving her body weight from left to right and back again. A nervous habit she was developing, I thought at the time. Come to find out it was the effect of the strong medications she had been given during her assessment in the same mansion as we now stood.

We talked, the conversation mostly about the weather and the beautiful trees, anything other than what was about to happen. To our left, there were big double doors, locked for what I first thought was the safety of the people inside, but soon realized it was meant to keep visitors safe from what went on inside the doors. The lock turned and a nurse in a crisp, starched white uniform approached us. Wearing the short white cap atop her hair, she was the picture of perfection. She was there to take Ms. Jessie. Already standing right next to Mama, I reached for her and put my arms around her, held on tightly while she stood limp and patted me on the back three times. Always three times. No more, no less. A strange ritual of sorts. I was crying, hard, and so was my aunt, but Mama just told us not to worry. "Don't worry it'll be alright, Carol" Mama told us. The officer had left after the nurse came into the room which meant our visit was over. There would be no long goodbyes.

I had so many questions. Where was Mama going? How would we know where she was? How would we know if she was alright? When could we see her? We were told that Dr. Mendosa would be in touch and not to worry, just like Mama said. Even back then I knew it didn't matter how many times I was told not worry. This was my mama. She needed lookin' out for, always had and I was certain always would. How was I to know for certain someone at this faux plantation-home would do the lookin' out for my mama?

 Mama was different, there's no way around it. She was a wonderment to most people who met her, not just me. She had developed a sense of sarcasm and dark humor to shield her from reality and used this intellect often when she felt threatened that someone was getting too close. No one ever got close to Mama. Physically or emotionally. She just didn't seem to have what it would take to survive in an insane asylum. Five-footfour inches tall, hiding a dark secret that no one could see, not until the day our worlds crumbled and God left us wondering if He existed. I said goodbye to Mama there in that chamber or horrors. Mama. As the nurse took her away beyond double locked doors, I thought about Snookum and how he was probably at home drinking himself into a stupor. Bastard. Coward. He should be here instead of Mama. I wished him dead over and over. No one ever questioned who fathered the baby. Not before, during, or after the trial. Did that mean that everyone knew or were they just being polite? I doubted the latter but I couldn't let go how he stayed out of it all and got out unscathed.

We were in the car and I turned to look back at the big white building, getting smaller and smaller. Always looking behind me, just as J.W. thought I was doing when I was a child. But I had nothing to look forward to, I thought. Mama was in a mental institution and I was covered in scars, ones that no one could see so at least I would be able to keep them a secret, if I just built walls big enough.

Soon it became my time to be institutionalized, but not with Mama. Aunt Sissy would take me to Talmadge Memorial Hospital in Augusta, Georgia. Talmadge was a teaching hospital, with a wing devoted to a psychiatric ward which would be my new home. I was terrified but knew it was a better fate that what Mama suffered.

On the way to the hospital with Aunt Sissy, we went through the town of Thomson, where Mama, J.W., and I had lived. A state patrol car was coming towards us on the highway. As it got closer, I knew it had to be J.W. and started waving frantically. "Good Lawd, child! That patrol car is turning around! That's not J.W. but we're in trouble now!" Aunt Sissy said. Lights were flashing behind us so we dutifully pulled over and all got out on the side of the road. The state patrolman and I walked towards each other and as soon as I saw those eyes dark as coal, I knew it was him.

"Mornin' ladies, is everthin' alright?" He wasn't sure if he should be smilin' yet. There might be a situation here.

The first words out of my mouth were, "You don't know who I am, do you?" He replied, "Your face is awful familiar but..." I didn't let him finish his sentence before I blurted out, "J.W. it's me, Carol!" All of a sudden his big arms were around me and I was crying tears of happiness for the first time I could remember. I nuzzled my face into his shoulder and held on, never wanting to let go, but I had to. My aunt said, "Oh, my Lord, sweet Jesus," not believing it could have all happened. J.W. said I had grown so much he couldn't believe it and I was a very pretty young lady. Then his face changed and I saw the anguish and knew what was coming.

"I've been followin' what happened with your mama."

He and Aunt Sissy had a conversation where they only spoke to each other, like I wasn't there or had become deaf for a few moments. I tried not to pay attention since I knew what they were talking about and only heard the words Talmadge hospital, which brought me back from my trance. My stepfather and I hugged again and we headed back on our way. I would never see him again but his warmth would stay with me forever.

Being admitted to Talmadge was a process of interviews with doctors to see if you *qualified* for their program. I spilled the whole shebang with one outburst. The doctor thought I was making it up. Evidently he didn't read newspapers. He excused himself to speak with Aunt Sissy and returned saying they could admit me pronto.

Aunt Sissy and I left the hospital and headed back to Atlanta. All the way there she told me how this was going to be good for me. "Afta what you've been through with Jessie, the Good Lawd knows yor gonna need help." She tried to convince me none of this was my fault, I did the right thing calling the police, and I couldn't live blaming myself for any of it. These words were paraded in front of me every few days by someone in the family. It seemed they had all decided if they used this mantra it would help me cope and get to normalcy quicker. It was kind but words can only heal surface wounds.

She dropped me off at my cousins' house and they knew it had been a hard day for me. Once again they were waiting with lots of hugs. I only had two more weeks to spend with them before I left for the hospital. It was the only time I had ever lived with a true, caring family and would miss it dearly.

As Uncle Austin and I arrived at Talmadge, I could see it was much different from the place Mama was in. This was a regular-looking hospital sitting in town, as opposed to a faux mansion on acres and acres of land. There was nothing to distinguish it from any other hospital so it must be a good place, I thought. We went to a desk where a receptionist sat and we told her we were there for my admittance to the psychiatric ward. In her most pleasant voice, smiling all the while, she said she would call someone to meet us right where we stood. A few minutes passed and a crisp white uniformed nurse met us, just like at Mama's place. She introduced herself and said Uncle Austin could come with us while she kindly gave us a tour of where I would be staying.

We took the elevator to the third floor, all of us being quiet, not sure how to behave. It was very unusual for my uncle to be quiet. He spent his days making jokes about everything in every situation, but not this one. The elevator came to a stop facing a short hallway with big double doors. As we approached them, the nurse reached for keys from her pocket. The doors were locked and this left me feeling a little anxious. Once through the doors, we encountered another set of very wide doors which were also locked. More anxiety crept in as I had never been locked up before and wondered how Mama felt when it happened to her. After getting through the second set of doors, we walked into a hospital setting with a nurses station on the right and a long corridor straight ahead. We were informed by our tour guide that patient rooms took up the entire hall way except for the first room on the right, which was the TV room. We stood and looked inside as three patients sat and intently watched a soap opera of the era, *Dark Shadows.* No one looked our way so we continued on down the hall. At the end was a large room with a pool table that no one was playing on that day but four patients sat in chairs along the wall and seemed to be having a conversation about the downfall of society. As we turned to go back the way we came and made a right turn at the nurses station , I noticed a piece of paper taped to one of the patient rooms that read "Due to lack of interest, tomorrow has been canceled." I knew I wanted to meet that person. On the left was what the nurse called a cubby hole; a small place surrounded by three walls with the open side next to the corridor. It held eight chairs, two rows of four facing each other, and was a place to meet new friends and get acquainted with the others, she said. There was one woman sitting there. She was maybe in her thirties with very short dark hair. Her body was in constant motion not from disease, I would find out later, but from medication. Her teeth were clenched but when she did take a quick look at us, her mouth opened a bit and the corners were oozing sticky white glue. The nurse the concern on our faces and quickly dismissed it as a problem with medication that they were working on. Continuing down the hallway, again we saw patient rooms on both sides and at the end another large room with a piano and chairs. This was the *entertainment* room and anyone could play the piano, cards, puzzles or whatever they wanted. We turned back and were facing the nurses station, although it seemed a long way off from where we stood. We walked towards it and for the first time I noticed a set of doors next to the station that I hadn't noticed before. They were pointed out to us, once it was obvious we had noticed them, and we were told there were more patient rooms down that hall but they were reserved for special needs. Um hum. I won't be one of those patients.

My uncle had yet to give the pint of blood as promised, the only payment required for my admittance, so he would do that while the nurse helped me settle into a room. I had brought a suitcase and was told at the beginning that the length of my stay would probably be about three months. My room was on the left, immediately behind the cubby hole. I had a roommate that I would meet later but, in the meantime, the nurse asked me to open my suitcase. She went through everything one by one and immediately took the razor from me. "How do I shave my legs?" I asked rather indignantly. "You can check out a safety razor once a week" she said, politely. We kept on with unpacking and putting my clothes in the dresser with one mirror that I shared with my roommate. There was a ceiling light, no lamps, and nothing on the walls except faded brown paint. This was a common theme throughout the ward, since patients could hang themselves with cords or use light bulbs to cut themselves. We sat down so the nurse could ask me some questions. Did I take drugs and, if so, when and what was the last thing I had;

emergency contact information (I thought I was already in a hospital so why would they need that?); last time I had a drink of alcohol, and on and on. She then informed me that Dr. Ward would be my doctor and he had already prescribed some medication that we would go to the nurses station and get now.

I was given three pills and didn't know what any of them were or what they would do to me. "They would just make you feel more comfortable," I was told. Uncle Austin reappeared, showing the Band-Aid on his arm, and asked how I was feeling. I could tell he was feeling much better and was making jokes about giving his pint and having to refill later. Actually, I was starting to get a little drowsy, I confessed. He used this as his reason to leave and go back to Atlanta but assured me the family would be down to see me soon, after I got settled. I only wanted to lie down and sleep.

Chapter 11

*Dr. Ward, My Savior*

I slept through until the next morning's wake up call. We all had to get up at the same time and some people were allowed to eat outside the ward in the cafeteria while others had meals brought to them. On this day my food was brought to me mainly because Dr. Ward was waiting to see me after breakfast. Since I was told I had a roommate, I wondered why I hadn't seen her yet. The nurses told me she would be back with me tonight. That was all the information I got, which I would learn was standard operating procedure.

I was escorted to Dr. Ward's office, which was right outside the first set of locked doors.

I knocked softly at the door. "Come in" said a voice. I pushed the door and it swung wide open, propelled by the nervous energy I was feeling, Suddenly, my T-shirt felt too thin for the temperature of the room.

I stood in the door way and scanned the office. He sat directly in front of the door at the outside wall with a window behind him. Next to my left arm was a leather chair which was across the room from his desk, an end table to the left of that, and then a big leather couch that took up most of the wall that ran perpendicular to the chair and end table. The right side of the room was reserved for plaques and pictures on the wall displaying his degrees and certificates.

I met the gaze of the doctor, who had lifted his head to see me. He had dark hair and eyes and as he stood up from his desk, his six foot frame became apparent. Younger than I thought he would be, he appeared to be in his late thirties. He walked around the desk to introduce himself and was dressed in dark slacks, dress shirt and sweater vest. The soft leather tassel loafers he wore caught my eye and I thought of someone who had money and privilege. His good looks were unmistakable but for some reason I was afraid as he reached out to shake my hand. He dismissed my escort and told her he would let her know when we were done.

He asked me to take a seat and I promptly sat as far away from him as I could, which was in the chair next to the door.

"Is there a reason you want to sit all the way across the room? Are you afraid of something?"

"I don't know. Why?" I asked.

"Well, usually I sit in that chair and my patients sit on the couch."

"Oh." I got up from his chair and moved to the couch. "Am I supposed to lie down?"

"Up to you," he answered with a smile that brightened my mood if not my life.

Dr. Ward began trying to break the ice by telling me he was married, had no children, started as a doctor in the emergency room, and then decided on psychiatry.

"What would you like for me to know about you?" he asked. I replied rather flippantly that I presumed he already knew everything about me since he was my doctor.

"Well, you're not going to make this easy are you?" He proceeded to tell me what the drugs were that he had prescribed and that since most people come to these places with preconceived notions, the drugs them adjust to the environment.

"What if I don't want to adjust to your environment?"

"Well, that's enough for the day so let's get you back to the ward and we will get together again soon," he said.

Going to his phone he called the nurse to come back and get me so I stood up. He sat down at his desk and began to write.

"Is that about me?" I asked. "No, it's to remind myself of my golf game next week." He didn't meet my eye. It didn't occur to me he might have been trying to get another smile out of me. Instead, I wondered how I was supposed to relate to a man who wore tasseled loafers and played golf, for gosh sake.

I took medication three times a day; morning, noon, and night. Some patients took it more or less than that, depending on their psychosis, I guessed. At bedtime, we were all called to the nurses platform to take our happy sleepin' pill. During the day, I had met my roommate, Emily. She was about my age, taller than me with dishwater brown hair cropped close to her head. Emily was thin and pale and couldn't look me in the eye. She kept to herself and never spoke to anyone or even looked up from the floor. Her own nightmare was circling in her head and she didn't worry that anyone else would see it because she never opened her eyes to anyone. It was locked tightly inside. It was immediately evident that she belonged here and I found out a lot of other people did too. I guess I was one of them.

As I entered Dr. Ward's office for the second session, I intentionally sat closer to him to let him know I wasn't completely unavailable. We warmed up to each other slightly as I talked about everything except what had happened to Mama and since he was aware of it, there really was no reason to discuss it. Just like my roommate, Emily, my dread was locked tight. Instead we talked about how I felt about my situation, being in an institution, and what patients I had met so far. Just like our first meeting, the session was over quickly and we both got up and approached the door. As we did so, Dr. Ward very unexpectedly put his arms all the way around my back, but ever so gently. I pulled away instinctively, at which time he commented that he knew I wasn't used to being hugged or shown affection. Bully for you, Doc.

Since things had happened back in Swainsboro and with Mama being tried for murder, I had become very angry. I was ready to pick a fight with anyone and ready to try anything that would take me away from inside my own head. I had no friends and no one who gave a damn about me, so as logic goes for an eighteen year old, why should I care about anything or anyone?

It was Friday and I had been in the hospital for a week meeting a few people in the mixed gender ward where I stayed; Billy, a very tall young man, early twenties, cute, and able to play the piano like a pro, (he was the one who left the paper taped on the door) Steve, who was shorter but built like a marine, not too talkative, but pleasant, and the enormous fat lady who had been brought in on a stretcher and put into a bed. She was so heavy they had taken her down to the dock and weighed her on the truck scales, which meant she had to weigh over three hundred pounds but speculation was closer to six hundred. She wasn't allowed even a piece of gum since it contained sugar and the plan looked like it was to keep her medicated and feed her very little. The door to her room was left closed and only nurses and doctors went in and out. All of us would try and take a peek when we noticed the door was left open a tiny bit.

Finally, Friday night came, and it was time for meds and bed. Emily and I said goodnight to each other and that was about as far as our conversations went. The next thing I remembered was a doctor shaking me, telling me to wake up. I strained to open my eyes but it was too hard. He continued to shake me and started asking what I had taken.

"Nothin', nothin'" was all I could manage to say.

Sometime later it happened again. Being shaken by the doctor, asking questions like before, telling me to wake up but he was also asking me what day it was. I had no idea and didn't care. I just wanted to be left alone so I could sleep.

"I didn't take anything so just LEAVE ME ALONE," I demanded. He finally did.

Monday morning came and, without delay, I was taken to see Dr. Ward. I had awakened all on my own and felt quite refreshed. Entering his office I could feel the dark eyes looking me up and down. What was he lookin' for? Did I put my clothes on backwards? No, I checked and everything was as it should be.

"Have a seat," came the words from behind the desk, but kinder than I expected.

I sat down on the couch, which would become my usual place in his office. Dr. Ward said he was told that I went to sleep Friday night and didn't wake up until this morning. I told him that was correct as far as I could remember but it was rather annoying to have someone trying to wake me up several times. The doctor on call was the culprit, and he had called Dr. Ward at home to let him know they couldn't wake me. Everyone was concerned, except for the doctor who knew me best.

"You've been through too much and exhaustion set in, not only in your body, but your mind too," explained Dr. Ward.

The on-call doctor was young and Dr. Ward said he was going to speak to him about situations like this. The hospital was concerned that I had taken a drug I'd hidden but he knew the nurses didn't let things like that get by them so it wasn't a concern. Just exhaustion, he repeated.

"How do you feel now after you slept for over two days?" Dr. Ward asked. I told him I felt rested, rejuvenated, recharged.

"Good, so what can we talk about today?"

"I had dreams, bad dreams. Dreams I've had before."

"Tell me about them."

"There are bodies lying down, usually three. It is dark but I can see that the bodies have no heads."

"Are their heads cut off or just missing?" he asked.

"I don't know. I've never been able to get close enough to see. When I start to get near them I get really scared and wake up."

He asked how long I had been having this dream and I told him for as long as I could remember. It was one of two. The other one was two white ghosts like forms that were just there, in my dream, scaring me and waking me up. When I was little and we lived with Grams, I would wake up screaming sometimes from the dreams.

"Were you breast fed?"

"NO, jeez, why would you ask that?"

"Just curious. Sometimes children who are breast fed have similar dreams." he said. "Was Grams your grandmother?"

I was still thinking about the breast-fed question.

But the conversations began and seeing Dr. Ward three times a week made it easy for him to pry just a little more every time.

I wondered how Mama was doing with her doctor and how often she got to see him. I wasn't aware at the time how bad things were at Central State, but later I would hear the rumors and learn things that made me more afraid for her.

At the hospital new people kept showing up and a few had left. There was Sherri, who was sixteen and had long brown hair, was average height, but tiny like a dancer. We hit it off and she began to tell me her story; she was a sex addict. She liked boys but loved sex and she didn't care who knew it, especially the boys. Her parents had put her in the hospital, hoping the doctors could curb her addiction. The sex started right away. On our mixed ward there were young boys and older men who found her extremely attractive, and even more so after they found out about her addiction. Sherri began to disappear for short periods of time and I learned she was having sex with anyone she could in the hall bathrooms, closet, corners, or just anywhere she was able. Surprisingly, Sherri was not discussed much among other patients, nor was anyone else. There was a code of honor, an unspoken rule whereby it was understood by everyone that we all had issues we were dealing with, different issues, and we were all there for a reason. No one was worse off than anyone else. There was never much talk about other patients among the patients themselves.

Those of us who were found to be trustworthy were allowed to leave the hospital in groups of two or more for a couple of hours at a time. One day Sherri asked if I wanted to go out with her the next day, since we both had passes for a couple of hours. Why not? We went to a very expensive shop where I was admiring everything on the racks and the mannequins were dressed like superstars. It was the 1960s, and even the mainstream had followed the trend of maxi and mini dresses, *Jesus* sandals, which were soft natural leather that wrapped around the ankle and crisscrossed over the top of the foot, and Nehru jackets with madras print and matching pants. I saw one on a rack. It was brown with swirling colors of beige and darker brown and I caught myself talking out loud about how it was the coolest thing I had ever seen.

"We'll buy it" I heard Sherri say.

"You are crazy. I don't have any money, much less money for something this expensive."

Sherri replied with her toothy grin, "I have my parents' credit card. We can get it." She said it just as a matter of fact like there was nothing wrong with it. Even I thought she was sexy.

"No, you don't understand. I can't pay for this, ever."

"It's ok," she said.

As guilty as I felt it wasn't enough to stop me from letting her, or her parents, pay for my Nehru suit. I was super excited and could not wait to wear it.

We went back to our ward and were asked what we had in our bags. I could hardly contain myself, wanting to show my new outfit that would make me look like everyone else who had money. Sherri had purchased several pieces of clothes for herself, mostly panties and bras, and the nurse asked if we had stolen any of it. Sherri smiled and handed her the receipt for everything and off to our separate rooms we went, smiling all the way. It was a good day.

Sheri wasn't the only girl I had a connection with. A few days after our shopping trip, a girl named Ricki showed up. She was taller than me, about five foot six, slim with long hair, just like the rest of our generation. She was pretty and very quiet. She kept to herself and barely spoke, but there was something about her that was intriguing to me. She was different in a world of people all trying to be the same. I spoke to her and she was polite but seemed to have no interest in having a conversation; I knew it wasn't just me, it was anyone. I felt a strange need to want to know more about her, but I doubted it would happen.

Some people wandered the halls with no light in their eyes. You just knew there was no reason to speak to them. They wouldn't see you or hear you. Never before in my life did I know people or places like this existed. Was this what the word crazy meant? There were so many different kinds of crazy but everyone was on the same playing field and treated the same. Something else I didn't understand. Weren't there degrees of separation? I had so much to learn.

Our days in the ward were planned most of the time. We had crafts we had to do; making ashtrays in ceramics, or creating The Lord's Supper on a piece of copper that had been traced over a mold. We also made pot holders woven on a small loom, clay characters of birds, beasts, and assorted other designs. Occupational therapy time was mandatory unless your doctor had excused you.

My visits with Dr. Ward were consistently three times a week, unlike Mama, whom I had found out wasn't getting any help at all. There were patients in my ward who had spent time in Milledgeville and the stories they told would scare anyone. Mama had been thrown into the lion's den to fend for herself and I hoped her mandated time there would be short. Dr. Ward continued to press me for information and I just continued to talk about now, not the past. It was still too painful and I wanted to forget it, keep pretending it didn't happen. Maybe things would get better that way.

There was more testing for me; IQ tests and memory tests. Some were given by Dr. Ward and others by staff. Just a way to pass the time, I thought. Not a big deal. There was a test where I had to repeat numbers backwards to Dr. Ward and he said I had done more than any patient he had seen. He called in another doctor to witness. I recited eighteen numbers backward before I messed up. Both doctors seemed so excited. I just thought they were ridiculous.

After a few weeks, the ward became my home and I actually felt comfortable there and my rapport with Dr. Ward had improved dramatically. I was beginning to trust him.

The staff did bed checks at night several times and would peek into our rooms with flashlights to check on us. I rarely ever noticed this and only became aware when I was told about it by a patient. For some reason one night the flashlight shone in my face and woke me up and I soon saw what the nurse was staring at with her wide opened mouth. My roommate's hospital-white sheets were crimson red. Was I dreaming? I knew I was not when the nurse's screams broke the night silence as she yelled for help. Emily had cut her wrists and was barely alive. She was quickly whisked out of the room in the same bed as she lay dying. I never saw her again. All the patients learned quickly what the limits of patience were with the doctors. If you got out of control you were most likely sent the hospital where Mama was. They could control you there with shock treatments, heavy medication and solitude. It was the place everyone tried to avoid but not all were able to. Emily must have been one of those. She was in for a bad time and would surely be disappointed when she found herself alive.

I didn't want to be one of those patients, and I wondered what sort of state Mama was in. She had been told that I was at Talmadge but we didn't have a way of communicating with each other. With Dr. Ward's help I started looking for a way to visit her and it gave me something to focus on.

"You had a bad experience last night. What do you remember about it?" the doctor asked.

I told him about seeing the gasping nurse and the red sheets and how they brought in a new bed with crisp new linens like nothing had happened. They just told me not to worry and go back to sleep. I was used to living in a pretend world so it made sense.

"Why are you shaking now?" he asked.

"I'm scared, scared that I won't be able to pretend long enough and reality might catch up to me."

"What else, besides last night, are you afraid of?"

So, there it was. I began to spill my guts, telling him everything that happened to me and Mama, like he didn't know. It was the first time the tears came since I had been in the hospital and they were not going to stop. Sobbing, sobbing, and more sobbing to where I had trouble catching my breath to speak. But I did speak and told him all that I saw in my head every day. The images of the baby in the green and white towel, the police and GBI occupying our house, Mama in jail, the trial, the students in the balcony and the sight of Mama being taken away by the nurse at CSH were images emblazoned in my brain.

Our session was extended that day and lasted for hours as I let go of the prickly pain that stuck within all my veins every day. It felt so good as if being freed, if only for a short time. We went into all the details that we could that first day of confession but I would need to visit the confessional many more times.

"When will this end? These nightmares, the visions, the guilt from testifying against my own mama?"

"The medication will help some but you will have to take it the rest of your life. Your anxiety is over-reaction to your depression, and you inherited some things from your mama."

I wasn't sure what he meant by inheriting things from Mama. The doctors had said Mama was crazy, the word used then, so did that mean I was crazy, too? I didn't want to take pills for the rest of my life to live in a happy place that wasn't real. At the same time, I didn't want to live in the real place, either.

"So my future is bleak?"

 "No, your future is up to you and after we discuss this more over the next few weeks, you will see how things will get better.  For now, let's call it a day, a good day."

I was exhausted and my body felt like putty that someone needed to mold into a shape that could stand up on its own. Just let me sleep but not on a cliff this time.

Chapter 12

*The Patients*

The nurses let me sleep undisturbed per Dr. Ward's orders, and I slept for fifteen hours. When I woke, I didn't feel refreshed, only tired still, and wanted more sleep which wasn't allowed. I walked the halls since he had excused me from crafting duties, and tried to shake myself out of the fog. Looking into the cubby hole, I saw Ricki. She was sitting alone twirling her long hair around one finger with her legs crossed, kicking her top leg up and down in a nervous motion. She was smoking a cigarette which was common for most of the patients, including me. I sat directly across from her and waited until she looked up to notice me. We said "hey" to each other and it was obvious she was nervous before I got there, so it wouldn't matter if I made things worse.

"What a crappy day," I started the conversation.

"Um hum."

After waiting for her to add something, which she didn't, I continued.

"How long have you been here?" I asked.

Pleasantly surprised by the fact that she was talking to me, I continued our initial greeting conversation. We went on about how long we had been there, discovered we had different doctors, talked about their characteristics, and all the things we liked and disliked about Talmadge. It felt like I might be making a friend. We were both happy that later that night, those of us who had passes were going to the drive-in movie to see *Bonnie and Clyde*, the movie about the most violent bank-robber couple in history. This was a real treat for everyone, and had been voted on during the last open session group meeting, which happened once a week. We were asked what we would like to do as a group and that was it: go to the drive-in movie. The staff took us shopping in groups at times, but this was a first.

Ricki and I parted for lunch and I headed down to the cafeteria. After standing in line and getting my food, I was looking for a place to sit when a young doctor in a white lab coat approached me.

"I know who you are and what you are, Carol," he said.

Startled, I asked who he was and how he knew my name. He said his wife had met him for lunch one day and saw me. She was from Swainsboro and told him what had happened to me and Mama. I wondered who his wife was since he didn't volunteer her name. Was she a school mate or a spectator during the trial?

"Your mother is a murderer and you're nothing but a whore. You're both disgusting."

Shaking almost out of control, I dropped my plate on the table and headed back up to the third floor. The nurses saw me and asked what had happened. I couldn't tell them, it was too embarrassing and demeaning. It was best to pretend this didn't happen and keep it to myself. If I told someone, they might feel that way, too. My heart ached and my head was spinning. I might get sick. Without telling me they called Dr. Ward. Next thing I knew he was demanding to know what had happened and I told him. He asked for the name of the doctor and I was able to tell him since I had seen the doctor's name tag. Dr. Ward scurried out of the room like he was headed to put out a fire. He didn't say anything to me about where he was going or what he was doing. I stayed in my room crying. A few short minutes later Dr. Ward entered my room.

"He had no right to speak to you like that and it won't happen again." He said this in his always-calm voice. Not much seemed to rattle Dr. Ward.

My hero had taken care of me. More and more I relied on Dr. Ward for my feelings of self worth. I truly believed he cared for me and wanted to take care of me like he had just done. A few days later I was back in the cafeteria and saw the young doctor again. He glanced my way with a look of loathing that told more of a story than he knew. I smiled at him with the look of a winner. I had never had anyone stand up for me, just me, like that before. As bad as the situation had been, I felt closer to my doctor.

The night came and we all lined up to go to the movie. The staff had gotten together four cars with each one carrying four to five patients, and off we went. It had to be dark to go to the drive-in so it was already eight o'clock, which meant we would all be out after our bedtime of ten. We were allowed to get a soda pop and popcorn—what would a movie be without it—but were told we had to be well behaved or we would leave. Getting a bunch of patients together from a mental ward had to be quite challenging in the least and probably a little scary for the staff. We sat through the pre-movie cartoons and the movie started. Not too long into the movie Bonnie and Clyde had a shootout and that brought on the first scream from one of the cars. Another one came after that with shouts of, "I can't take it, I can't take it!" One by one our cars starting pulling out of the drive-in to go "home." We had a couple of war veterans and patients who had experienced extremely violent acts, and the movie scene had been more than they could handle. We all felt sorry for them but at the same time were perturbed that we were going to miss the movie.

Back at the hospital, the traumatized patients were given shots of Thorazine, the drug of choice for traumatic episodes. The shots were given in the hip and took effect quickly, so quickly that you had to get to bed right away. Everyone did the Thorazine shuffle off to bed and all was well in the institution once again.

Morning came and the cubby hole was busier than I had ever seen it. The conversation was all about last night and how the movie looked like it would have been good. Not a big deal. After all, we were living in a hospital ward of disturbed people so we expected setbacks.

Days went by and I was feeling closer to Dr. Ward. The hugs I got at the end of every visit were still uncomfortable but less so than before. We were making progress in our therapy sessions, he said, and I may only have to stay another few weeks. This was concerning as I thought I could not leave him.

I looked for Ricki every day. One day while she was out on a pass, she cut her arms with a razor blade and then asked a policeman to take her to the hospital. He brought her in and I saw her, crying, confused, and maybe even regretting what she had done to herself. Doing something like that had never entered my mind, but I learned a lot of things I shouldn't have in the crazy place.

Soon Ricki was nowhere to be found. I asked around and of course no one knew but there were whisperings that she had been sent to Milledgeville. After talking to other patients in the ward I had learned more about CSH, and not pleasant things. Ricki was an example; if you didn't want to go to Milledgeville, be good and don't mess up. The urge to see Mama became overwhelming.

Getting in touch with an old friend in Swainsboro turned out to be easier than I had expected. I asked to use the pay phone and had the number of a boy who had always been a friend and nothing more. His name was Johnny and he was a kind person who knew Mama but would never gossip or whisper like others. Dr. Ward had cleared it for me to visit Mama for a day and Johnny was taking me there.

She was in the Holly building, Wing 3, as I had learned from Dr. Ward. It had only been about two months since we dropped Mama off, but this time we drove around the big main mansion to the back of the acreage where four-story red buildings lined the roads. Johnny didn't want to come in and said he would pick me up in a couple of hours. I walked alone into the main entrance, but not before looking up and seeing a third floor porch built off to the side of the big building. It was completely screened in with rocking chairs across the length of it. I knew Mama would have liked these since she had always had trouble being still.

Once inside, I jumped through all the hoops to see Mama. Who was I, who did I want to see, and where did I live. My address was Talmadge Memorial Hospital, Augusta, Georgia, and I was Ms. Jessie's daughter. That fact brought a few long looks but they were on their way to "bring her down."

She came shuffling towards me with a lit cigarette in hand and a smile. She was wearing a plain pale yellow cotton dress that hung straight from her shoulders, and bedroom slippers. Her shoulders were slumped and if she was surprised to see me, she didn't show it. It was obvious her hair had not been washed for several days and most of it was grey, since the auburn dye had grown out. Her nails were bitten off down to the skin. She looked beaten, not physically, but just worn down, like a prisoner of war that would cower in the corner. I was so happy, sad, excited, scared. I wasn't sure.

I put my arms around her and waited for the three pats on the back and was pleased when I felt them. That was as warm as Mama would ever get, but today it felt like God's hands were on me, if I believed in religion. I choked back tears and heard Mama say "What you doin' here?"

"I just wanted to see you, Mama. Remember Johnny? He brought me here."

"Oh yeah, I remember him. He's that sweet boy."

"Yes, Mama, that's him."

The crisp white uniform took us to a room with a cot to sit on. They let Mama have coffee and she had brought her pack of smokes. She told me my aunt and uncle had been to visit her, brought her cartons of cigarettes, and told her I was in the hospital, too. She asked how I liked it and what it was like. My thought was that maybe she was trying to compare our situations. I told her about Dr. Ward and said the place was ok for what it was. We talked about CSH and she told me she didn't see Dr. Mendoza much except when he walked through the building every day. She said they gave her a lot of pills but she had no idea what they were. There was the one thing we didn't talk about but I knew all along that we wouldn't. Since Dr. Mendoza had told us that Mama most likely didn't remember anything and it would probably be too traumatic for her to recall the events, I was careful not to broach the subject, as was the rest of the family. Forever.

Mama began to tell me about some of things that went on.

"Carol, it's just awful. These people! There's always screamin' coming from the rooms and some of these poor people don't even know where they are or who they are. One idiot thinks he's the President! Oh, Lawd."

Mama was trying her best to separate herself from "these people" but at the same time I knew she was empathetic and cared about them. She told me stories of young girls who had been there since they were teenagers and older women who had lived most of their lives there.

"It's all so sad" Mama said, showing her emotion the only way she could, emphasizing her words just at the right time. She shook her head back and forth to show her disbelief.

"Oh, I met a girl named Ricki and she said she knew you."

She was there! My mind immediately went to thinking about her and how she was in this horrible place.

"What did she say, Mama?"

"She said she came here from Talmadge and I told her I had a daughter there and she said she knew you. She shore is a pretty girl. So sad."

Mama had been sad for everyone for as long as I could remember. Whenever a celebrity died or someone she knew lost someone, it was like it was happening to her. She would spend days talking about how sad it was that such and such had to happen to so and so. I wondered how long Ricki would have to stay, how long Mama would be there and, when I asked, she said no one ever said anything about anyone leaving. We continued comparing hospitals and I felt guilty that I was in such a good place and hoped neither Mama nor Ricki would stay long in the house of horrors. Mama asked if I had heard anything about Sheila and I had no news. I didn't hear from anyone and it was another cross to bear for me. The guilt just kept piling on.

Two hours went quickly and Mama was escorted out by the white uniform and I went outside to find Johnny waiting for me. There was never anything between us but I thought he was a great friend, especially to do this for me. Johnny was quiet but asked how things went and how Mama looked. We talked but a short time and most of the trip was fairly quiet, giving me time to think about Mama and Ricki. He took me back to Talmadge and said he was going straight home, after asking if I wanted him to take me again to see Mama. What a sweet guy. I said next month would be great.

After returning to Talmadge I almost felt grateful, but guilty, that I was in such a better place than Mama or Ricki. We were all heavily medicated but not subjected to shock therapy and received actual treatment. Poor Mama and Ricki had shock treatments often, no therapy, kept extremely medicated and subjected to screaming patients and poor living conditions. I knew I would see Dr. Ward soon and we would talk about my trip to see Mama. I wondered more about my destiny and if I would eventually end up in that horrible place. Was it my fate, too?

"You're not crazy," he said.

He knew after I saw Mama I would be questioning my own sanity.

"Then what am I?"

I didn't know how to define myself anymore. Pregnant at fifteen, married at sixteen, abandoning my baby girl, testifying against my own mama in court all before I was barely eighteen had set the stage for my life. My aunt and uncle had visited me one time with my cousins and taken me to dinner. I had no brothers or sisters and was starting to feel abandoned myself. Where would I go from here?

I was feeling angry more and more. Angry with what had happened; angry with Mama for making it happen, angry for everything I had ever done or would do. I was even angry at the great doctor for thinking that he was great. I was sure he did. What made him think he could help me? Why did he even want to? I knew why; it was his job.

"You've lived a tragic life and have to learn to deal with it through talks with me and medication."

The great doctor had spoken.

"WHAT IF I DON'T WANT TO DEAL WITH IT? I'M TIRED OF TRYING TO DEAL WITH IT. I DON'T LIKE YOU OR THIS PLACE BUT I HAVE NO PLACE TO GO, DO I?"

I was screaming loudly. It was the first time I had shown any emotion since I had been in the hospital other than my crying spell.

"Go on."

"WHAT MAKES YOU THINK YOU'RE SO GREAT? YOU'VE LIVED A CHARMED LIFE, GRADUATED TOP OF YOUR CLASS, A CHILD PRODIGY WITH ALL THE PLAQUES ON YOUR WALL TO PROVE IT. I HATE YOU!"

I continued screaming. Finally I began to cry which made me even angrier.

"DAMN IT! I don't want to cry!"

"Afraid you'll feel something?" he said, but not in a patronizing way.

I heard a genuine concern in his voice, which surprised me. As I kept on screaming and crying, shouting obscenities, the next thing I felt were his hands pulling me from the couch. I pulled away trying to show him I didn't want him or need him. Gently he pulled me up from the couch and put his arms around me. I melted, letting everything go.

"We'll get through this," he said.

Did he say "we" as in him and me? I didn't know for sure but, for the moment, I was feeling comforted, which felt good but was still new to me.

Going back to my room again to cry it out, I was given an extra dose of something to help calm me down. Sleep was all I wanted anyway so I was alright with it all. I fought hard against those afternoon naps that Grams made me take every single day. Now I wished I could take one long nap all the time.

Chapter 13

*Living Quarters*

Morning came, again. Everyone was still there as far as I could tell and it was just another day in the crazy ward. After visiting Mama, I thought even more about her and Ricki and how, even though our lives had taken the same path, theirs was filled with so many more ruts. I should be grateful, I told myself.

Every day seemed the same except that Dr. Ward thought I was improving and should be able to move into a half-way house within a few weeks. A half-way house was a residence where about fifteen to twenty people lived at any given time. They included people like me transitioning from a hospital to the real world. That included prisoners, alcoholics, and drug addicts.

I had a few more breakdowns or breakthroughs and knew the time was coming for me to go. I had been at the hospital for six months and had seen Mama twice thanks to my friend Johnny. The second time seeing her was very much like the first except that she looked even more thin and beaten. Not physically, but mentally drained and drugged, worse than the first time I saw her. When I asked if she was having any kind of therapy, she let me know that she just ate and slept. The only good thing was the third story screened in porch with rockin' chairs. Mama said she and Ricki would sit outside and smoke cigarettes together and had spent a good amount of time becoming friends. Not only did Ricki smoke but she drank coffee, too, which made them two peas in a pod.

No one had said anything to her about leaving and, since she had nowhere to go, it really didn't matter. Things were the same for Ricki. We all felt the same about having no place to go.

I had seen Mama four hours in six months while both of us were hospitalized in a mental institution. No stigma there, I thought.

Dr. Ward took me over to the halfway house to give me a tour and introduce me to the house mother. It was the highlight of my visit. She was about five-foot-five inches tall, not thin but a good weight for her age which I guessed to be about fifty or fifty-five, Her crowning glory was her Lucille Ball red hair, twisted and pinned to the back of her head. The fair skin and freckles went perfectly with the rest of the picture. She came toward me with hand extended and mumbled something about how I must be special having my doctor bring me over. Dr. Ward smiled at her and gave her a look that let her know she had crossed a line. Without further ado she introduced herself as Mrs. VanDervender. I had never heard that name and didn't think it was very common to the South, but really didn't care. We started with the tour and were told the house was over a hundred years old. It was beautiful in its day and was another stately old Georgia mansion at one time. The staircase was made of petrified wood and the wood floors throughout the house were kept polished. The first thing that had appealed to me was the front porch with rocking chairs. I knew things would be more bearable because of it. The house had many rooms, but only one bedroom downstairs which would belong to Mrs. V. The upstairs was occupied by the residents who shared the five bedrooms and one bath. At that time there were ten patients and I would make eleven. There was a cook who came during the day and went home at night, called Ms. Martha. It was made clear to me that she was a cook and not a maid. I was handed the work detail sheet which everyone signed weekly for their house duties. Dusting, mopping, and cleaning the bathroom plus every night two people were designated to dry dishes after Ms. Martha had washed them.

Ms. Martha was a true southern black woman who was as friendly as a puppy dog. She didn't talk much but it was evident that she and Mrs. V. had a connection of friendship. Most of the residents were at school or out working during my visit that day so I only saw one enter the house. He didn't look at us or speak but fled quickly up the stairs and out of sight. Everyone pretended not to see him, including Dr. Ward.

Now it was set. As Dr. Ward drove me back to the hospital he said he wanted me to move into the house within the next week. I knew the moment was coming but I was still devastated. It would mean not seeing him in the halls every day or having therapy three times a week. I would take the city bus over once a week for sessions. I was very sad. He had become my strength and it scared me to leave him, but everybody leaves.

My first day at the half-way house was spent going over the rules of cleaning, who I would be sharing my room with, and curfew times. Curfew? Mrs. V. went to bed at 10:00 on the dot and that is when the doors were locked. Of course we weren't trusted with keys, so we'd better have our butts inside the door by 10:00 sharp or we'd slept outside!

I started meeting some of the other residents. The first was a young man who asked if I liked Star Trek.

"I suppose" I told him.

"Isn't Captain Kirk the best?" he said.

Um, ok so there were going to be some characters, I started to assume. The first girl I met wanted to let me know she liked girls, not guys. I told her I had never met anyone like that before but I didn't think it was contagious so it should be ok. Then she made me really laugh out loud and hard. She said we could always get a laugh at dinner out of V.D. When I looked at her face I knew exactly who she meant and would spend the rest of my time there trying to keep a straight face when I looked at Mrs. VanDervender: V.D.

I shared my room with two other girls who quickly told me there were thieves all around us. I should lock up my stuff, they told me, or someone would take it. It was the first time I learned that when I got a job, I had to start paying rent. Yippee.

After getting settled in, I started looking for a job. The goal was for me to start school soon at Augusta Business College but not for a few weeks. On job applications it was best just to put down your street address and leave it at that. If someone asked, you said you lived with roommates in an apartment. There was a new steak restaurant opening and I got a job there. It's also where I was introduced to marijuana for the first time and I loved it. It helped me forget.

I met new friends working at the restaurant and all of them smoked pot and did some kind of drugs. Soon I was lying about the hours I worked so I could go with my new friends to get high. Everything happened very fast, and before I knew it, I had a needle in my arm shooting up speed. Drugs sometimes made me forget the past but other times the past was just intensified. It was on such a day, after having a panic attack while doing speed, that I found myself at Talmadge Hospital wanting to be checked in, after only a few weeks at the half-way house. I was under twenty-one and had no one to sign papers for me, so the staff called Dr. Ward to come down. I was sitting in the small office when the doctor walked in. After one look at my eyes he asked if I was doing drugs. I just looked away and started to cry. He picked up my arm and saw the needle mark.

"Admit her to third floor," the angry doctor barked at the admissions lady.

"I can't. She doesn't have anyone to sign her in." she replied.

"I'm signing her in." He gave me a look that would peel paint. "You'd better know I'm putting my job on the line for you."

When Dr. Ward was angry, he didn't raise his voice; he raised his dark eyebrows and breathed deeply. Once again he was my savior and I knew it. Getting back to the third floor ward almost felt like home. Some of the same people were there but my biggest surprise was seeing Ricki. It made me happy to see her and I was glad to be back.

Ricki told me that she met Mama at CSH but didn't seem to want to talk about much more than that. She was even quieter than before and told me she had a lot of shock treatments in Milledgeville. She said she thought many people had them, including Mama. The thought of either of them going through the convulsions made me sick and I searched my mind for a way to forget I heard about this. Escapism wasn't just for magicians.

Back in therapy with Dr. Ward, everything seemed to be normal for me for the next few weeks. I was back on the hospital drugs for depression and anxiety and was reminded of the time I was told I would have to take them for the rest of my life. That just couldn't be true and was the one thing Dr. Ward was wrong about.

I was in and out of the hospital four times total over a year and a half. Each time I would smoke pot when I was out and always end up asking Dr. Ward to let me back in the hospital, which he did. I heard from my aunt and uncle a few times by phone but with them raising four children, I don't think they had much time for me. As far as they knew I was doing fine and they never knew about the hospital revolving door.

Dr. Ward was the best thing that happened to me at that time in my life and I never wanted to leave him, but I had to. The half-way house was my stop in between each hospitalization, except for the last. The last time I went directly to the YWCA. I had to share a room, which I didn't mind, but across the hall in a private room was someone I never expected to see again. It was Ricki and she was doing great and going to school. We spent more time talking but still went our separate ways after I met a girl named Kitty who was looking for someone to share an apartment with her. Kitty and I moved out of the Y after two months. I was still seeing Dr. Ward and the news didn't make him happy, since he knew I would be without any supervision again. Kitty and I both had jobs at restaurants and could afford a cheap one bedroom. I was still running from the past and Mama was still paying for the crime she didn't commit. The bastard, Snookums, was still alive and I spent too much time thinking about how I hated him.

We moved into a large old house that had been split into three apartments, common after the decline of large families over the decades. Our entrance was in the front of the house off to the side of a porch. Each room was directly behind the other one so you walked into the living area, then right behind that was the bedroom with a door that opened to the only bathroom and behind the bedroom was a small kitchen. Just one long room divided by two walls. Luckily the place came furnished and had two single beds, so Kitty and I shared the only bedroom which was not a problem. We got along really well. Kitty was barely five feet tall with the reddest of hair and an hour-glass figure. She kept her hair trimmed short since it was naturally curly and her height couldn't manage the look of it being much longer. She didn't want to look like a troll, she told me.

We had made some friends between the two of us and we all smoked pot and started dropping acid, as it was called, or LSD. Our apartment was never empty. We lived in Augusta, home to thousands of soldiers at Fort Gordon, and met fresh faces every weekend. Everyone came back to our place to get high after the clubs closed down. It was nothing to work all day, dance 'til two a.m., go home, smoke pot and just go to work without sleep. Our lives went on like this for a short time until Kitty suggested we move to Miami. She had a cousin there who we could stay with. Kitty talked her parents into paying for both of us to fly to Miami, so off we went. I was nineteen and accountable to no one. I could do anything, anytime, and no one cared because there was no one.

Miami was the hottest place I had ever been and I was severely sunburned the first day on the beach. It was a week before I could let clothes touch my burned body and I could look for a job. Kitty and I got a job at the same place, working the same hours, and we often walked to work together. We sold house cleaning services over the phone to the Miami rich. It was a lousy job but we met new people and there were a lot of Cubans there fleeing Castro. An interesting mix of personalities. I had never been around anyone who spoke Spanish and quickly learned ¿Hablas inglés? I thought it was mighty fine that I could speak a foreign language now knowing none of my old friends were able to do it. We took Latin in high school. Why? None of us really knew except that it was offered and was supposed to help us in our careers. I still don't get it.

We moved out of Kitty's cousin's place and got an apartment in the Cuban community. We could afford a place but it was not the safest. Being the only whites in the area, we were teased and picked on a lot. Our neighbor spoke little English but made some of the best food I had tasted. Growing up in Georgia all my life anything but fried chicken and greens was foreign to me, so when I had black beans and rice with spices I had never smelled or tasted I felt like I was in a strange land. It was delicious.

Miami was not the paradise we had hoped for or been told it was and we stayed for only a couple of months. We decided to go back to Georgia and try something else. Friends picked us up from the airport and had planned a coming home party for us. In those days it didn't take much to have a party. A plane landing with anyone on it could be a good reason. It was all about getting high and leaving the real world, if only for a few hours at a time. Vietnam was going on and our friends were leaving for the war daily. They always wanted to get together for a farewell, knowing we may never see each other again since they would go to their home state after the war; if they made it home.

We went to our friend's house for the party. There were about a dozen people there who had been smoking pot so we joined in to catch up. Soon there was a person going around the room holding their hand out to each individual and I quickly realized the person was handing out tabs of acid. When they got to me there were two tabs left so I took both. As soon as I swallowed them I heard the entire room saying "you took two"? What had I done, I wondered. I had dropped acid several times but it made me feel paranoid and I was always afraid I would think about the freezer and the baby and Mama. What had I done to myself now?

To say I had a "bad trip" was to put it mildly. I was hallucinating things from melting faces to worms crawling on the cake that was made for us. It was German chocolate and the coconut squirmed and crawled all over the cake. I was terrified, trying to hold myself together, not knowing what would happen or what I would do. I heard a train coming and as it passed by, I thought it was taking my mind with it. Anything real had left me and I knew it, but would it ever come back? Hours went by but I wasn't aware of it. My mind was locked and as people tried to reach me, I knew it was no use. I could not communicate but sat on the floor shaking from head to toe, thinking that I was surely crazy and this was the end of my life. The room looked ghostly, like the window was left open and fog crept in and filled it. It was all surreal. I was Alice in Wonderland, on an island.

"Are you alright?"

"Is she ok?"

"I heard her mumble something about a train taking her mind."

Even though I could hear the words, I was paralyzed and couldn't respond.

"Listen, the train is coming back. Can you hear it, Carol?" My friends began trying the simplest of things to get me to consciousness.

They decided to take me to get something to eat thinking it would help. Someone asked if they should take me to a hospital and the group responded no since they would all get in trouble. The Crystal restaurant stayed open all night and it was four in the morning. Kitty gave me a burger and after one bite I started throwing up.

"Good. Good. Now she'll get it out of her system."

Over ten hours had gone by and I was still hallucinating as the driver of the car drove us around with the windows down, trying to get fresh air to me. About six o'clock in the morning, Kitty decided we should check into a motel and look for an apartment after we slept. In the car was Kitty, three guy friends and me. We parked at the motel and went inside to the desk. Kitty said the two of us needed a room.

"Ok, what's your name?" the desk clerk asked, looking at me.

I started to panic. I didn't know what my name was so I looked around at my friends.

"Her name is Carol."

Thank God someone knew who I was, I thought. Carol sounds right. Yeah, that's it. Carol! I had no identity left except for a name.

Chapter 14

*John*

After about twelve hours Kitty woke me from the deepest of sleeps. The fog in my head had not completely lifted, but I knew my name and where we were. Kitty regaled me with stories of the night before and my memory was vague. My life and mind had been spared somehow, I felt, and I was grateful, vowing never to do LSD again. Pot was good enough and I had stopped taking the pills I would *need to take the rest of my life*. Oh my God. It's a blessin' for me that Grams was not watching me spiraling out of control like a space monkey.

I reminded myself often that everyone left and there was no need to have any relationships other than occasional friends. Mama was still in the hospital and it had been a year since I had seen her. There was no joy in my life, no stability. Now I knew that love would never come to me and if it did, I would push it away in time. My aunt and uncle had no idea where I was or who I was with. Did they even care, I wondered. They were the only family I had but we had nothing in common and I was sure, to them, I was just a wild child.

Kitty and I thought we would check out our old apartment to see if was available. There was a guy there named John and I fell in lust immediately, again. Dark hair, brown eyes; the complete opposite of my blue eyes and blonde hair. He was about five foot ten with muscles that bulged through his T-shirt. We exchanged a few words and said maybe we would see each other again. He was living in our old apartment with several other guys so we all smoked a joint before Kitty and I left to look for a different apartment.

We found a four-story house where lots of people were living and not paying rent. No one knew who owned it but no one seemed to care and people just moved in and stayed. We did the same. A week later I ran into John. We flirted, a lot, and before you could say scat, we were at my place rolling in the sheets. The same feelings I had for Ronnie were all there so it must be love. We never left each other after that night and fell into the local hippie crowd. Drugs and more drugs. Stoned day and night. John was in the Army but was AWOL, absent without leave, but during the Vietnam war years, many soldiers did the same. It wasn't unusual, for any reason. Our relationship was doomed from the beginning. I would never trust him, not because he gave me a reason, but because I no longer trusted any one. I knew I was an outcast by my own doing. Things, and people, were safer at a distance and the further away the better. The sense of foreboding overwhelmed me, as I knew it was a matter of time before disaster struck. I made sure of it by creating it when it wasn't there. I sabotaged my own life, my well-being, but it was out of my control. Pregnant at fifteen, having a baby at sixteen, a tragic event at seventeen, watching Mama on trial for her life and time in a mental ward all before I was eighteen warped my mind beyond any semblance of normalcy. The people close to me were the ones who would pay for it and I made sure of that. Always accusing, never trusting, pushing them away and pulling them back a moment later. There wasn't anyone who could fix this Rubik's cube brain of mine and I didn't want them to. I was alone on my island and I liked it that way. The more miserable I was, the better I liked it. I would punish myself over and over, year after year. It was the right thing to do.

We made a few friends, potheads like us, and soon it was what the hell, let's go to California. It was the happening place in the late 1960s and where everyone wanted to be. Hanging out by the ocean, getting high, and living off of, well, nothing. My aunt and uncle had been keeping Mama's old white Ford so John and I took the bus to Atlanta to pick it up. Aunt Roxie and Uncle Austin thought I was doing fine and they liked John, but I dared not tell them what we were about to do. It was the first I had seen of them in over a year.

Mama was still in the hospital and it was going on two years. We hadn't seen each other for over a year and it felt like we were losing touch with each other. If she had known what was going on in my world, she would have been worried. I was not taking the prescribed drugs but instead just smoked pot when I could, which was every day. I had taken LSD again with bad results. This time I saw the baby wrapped in the green and white towel. Afraid of losing my mind, I decided not to do acid again. I eventually told John about the baby, Sheila, and everything else. Feeling I had to be very careful of telling anyone about my past, it was especially hard for me to tell John. Would he leave me, think I was crazy, think Mama was crazy? These were the reasons I would always have to keep things to myself, never letting anyone know that I had almost lost my mind. Afraid of myself, afraid of what I might do, I lived every day in fear, of myself. Often I pushed the thought of suicide from my mind and that scared me, too. Had Mama thought about suicide? She was still in the hospital and I tried not to think about her, Sheila, or the past, but I had no future either.

It was the end of 1969; I was twenty years old and relying on getting high every day with John. We didn't work but managed to buy and sell enough pot to make money to live on. The five of us had raised enough money this way to pay gas to get to L.A., the place every hippie in America wanted to be. La-la land.

We drove across country for three days and made it to California by the skin of our teeth with just enough money for gas and gas station food. Somehow, we all got jobs right away. I was cleaning apartments, John was doing carpentry and the other three went their own way. La-la land was not the land of opportunity we thought it would be. There were so many of us everywhere we all blended and everyone looked the same. Long hair, bell-bottom pants, tie-dyed shirts, rings on our fingers and bells on our toes. The police would randomly select hippies to harass. At least we looked at it that way. With John being AWOL we were afraid of getting caught so he decided to go back to Illinois where he was from, and turn himself in. The army had been to his mother's home looking for him, which was not good for anybody.

John and I didn't have much money; therefore, we decided to hitchhike to Illinois. It wasn't odd in those days, everyone was doing it. We started out of L.A. and went north to avoid the desert, through Reno, over to Jackson Hole, Wyoming, then north, then south, or whatever way the driver was going. When you're hitchhiking you don't always have a choice of direction. We had great rides from a semi-driver, from a doctor who treated celebrities like Andy Williams, to just a good ole boy who went out of his way for us. Each person that picked us up was kind and usually bought us a meal. A week of strangers, cars, trucks, semis, napping until the next ride and a bite to eat when we could get it. We never stood on the road too long with our thumbs out. Rides came easy and pretty quickly. We made it to John's mother's house in Illinois in about a week. John's brother had served a tour in Vietnam and thought it was a good idea for John to face up to what he had done. He took John to Chicago where the process began. He was court-martialed and sentenced to three months in a military prison. I took a Greyhound bus from Chicago to Savannah and it took twenty-four hours. I probably could have thumbed my way quicker.

I had spoken to my aunt and uncle a couple of times when I needed money, and found out Mama had gotten out of the hospital. It was the beginning of deinstitutionalization where psychiatric hospitals started releasing patients to smaller, community-run mental health services. Mama was part of the first wave of patients to be moved to Savannah, Georgia, into a smaller facility. She was soon allowed to get a job and a place of her own but still had regular therapy sessions and took medication. She took medication her entire life. She had been locked up for three years with *lunatics, idiots, and epileptics.*

The taxi turned down Fifty-Fifth Street, a nice older neighborhood with ranch-style brick houses and oak-lined sidewalks. A magnolia tree dotted the landscape here and there, just as a reminder it was the Deep South, and the Spanish moss was a dead giveaway, as was the smell of the Georgia pines. We turned off Fifty-Fifth into a driveway but drove up to the back of the house. There in front of me was a large white garage with Mama's address numbers above a screen door. The garage still had room for two cars, but the third stall had been converted into an apartment: one big room that barely had space for a bed, TV, and couch in the front room. A kitchenette and bathroom made up the rest of the place. The garage had space above it for another apartment, which was not being used at the time. The original main house, which sat off to the right and in front of the garage, was a large story-and-a-half, three bedroom red brick, which was made into two apartments: one up, one down. The house was landscaped with shrubs and flowers of every color which grew everywhere. The live oak in front towered over the house with a commanding presence.

Mama suddenly appeared at the door with a smile on her face and a cigarette in her hand.

"Well, look at you, Miss California!" she said with a bit of sarcasm and a smile.

We both laughed as I got my things and paid the cabbie. Once inside, I wondered how we could both stay in this tiny place, but it would be easy to make the couch mine after sleeping in cars and buses many times. I reached out and put my arms around my mother as I looked her over for any signs of change or transformation. It wasn't a surprise to get three pats on my back but I wanted so much more. I wished she would hold me and squeeze me like Aunt Roxie did but I knew she couldn't. She was stooped over and not standing erect as she did when she was married to J.W. Of course she was smokin' up a storm and had coffee on the stove even with it being a hundred degrees outside. Someone had dyed her hair and it was back to the auburn color she always liked. When I was a teenager we would get a box of hair dye at Woolworth's five-and-dime store and spend a Saturday afternoon making her hair that auburn color. A couple of weeks later I would give her a Toni home perm, which took a few hours of another Saturday. The skirt she was wearing was too big and her blouse only partially tucked in. She had never learned to put on makeup and left that for me to do whenever she needed it for a work party or other occasion. Perhaps from smoking or just her past environment, she looked much older than she was. Her face was wrinkled and leathery as if she had spent too much time in the sun. I knew she had endured a lot and I tried not to show the emotion I was feeling of wanting to embrace her for a long time.

Mama got her coffee and ashtray and sat on the edge of the twin bed. I sat down on the couch facing her, not sure of where to start or what to say. It was obvious we were both nervous after not seeing each other for over a year and wondering what had happened to the other. Had Mama been abused? Did she ever remember what happened? I knew Mama was happiest when there was a crisis as long as it was happening to someone else. At times, it was almost a celebration of sorts, being able to be outside of her own mind and think of someone else's dilemma. She could talk about it for hours or if warranted, for days. Poor so and so, she would say. That's just awful that those terrible things that had to happen to Ms. or Mr. whoever!  Even if it was a celebrity, a movie star, a writer, or someone she had seen on TV or a magazine, Mama felt "so sorry" for them. She told me sometimes that she "just couldn't stop thinking 'bout poor Mr." whatever their name might be. Like Grams, Mama worried about everyone that she didn't know.

"Carol, what made ya'll go to California?"

I gave her a brief explanation and told her I was in love with John.

"Is he cute?" It was the important thing to Mama, but only for me evidently, as the last man she was with was an ugly bastard.

Then out of nowhere:

"Carol, do you remember that preacher we had in Swainsboro? He moved out o' state and got arrested for murder! Ya just neva know."

That was Mama; unable to say on track or maybe not wanting to. I talked about getting a job and she told me she was working at a restaurant and took the bus every day back and forth to work. The place she worked was a very famous and well-known seafood restaurant and I was sure she made good tips. That made me feel better.

Eventually I told her John might possibly be coming to Savannah, and she was thrilled that she would meet him. Then she dropped the bombshell. She was seeing a man who had two sons so she stayed at his house a lot, which would leave the tiny place for me and John. I was afraid of Mama being with a man. I didn't want her to be with a man knowing she couldn't love or be loved; it just seemed logical not to get involved in a relationship. I knew she didn't like any of the physical things as she would shrug and shake her head when it was mentioned, like it put a bad taste in her mouth.

 I didn't have to wait long to meet the new man and once again she had chosen someone that I couldn't fathom. He was under six feet tall and close to being obese. Wearing a T-shirt and jeans with suspenders, he looked like a pig farmer. I didn't know or care what he really did and hoped he would not be too long in Mama's life. At least his two sons, about thirteen and sixteen, were polite in the southern way. Was Mama punishing herself by being with this type of man? She had always attracted lookers, other than the bastard, but her looks had changed dramatically over the three years of confinement. I could barely look at his face and felt sick just talking to him, hoping he would leave very soon. They were off to his place and I didn't know when I would see either one again.

Once I knew for sure that John was coming to Savannah, I could hardly wait to smother him in kisses and feel his strong arms around me. It was all I lived for, with Mama working and staying at Big Boy's house. That was the name I gave her new boyfriend. Soon I got a job at a different restaurant and it helped pass the time until John arrived. My life would be perfect then.

Chapter 15

*Life Changing*

In the middle of the summer, John arrived at the apartment and it was like a scene from a movie. I was walking up and down the street, waiting for the city bus to drop him off at the corner two blocks away. The bus stopped every twenty minutes but I didn't see him. I would turn and walk towards the apartment, hoping he was on the next bus. I walked out to the sidewalk and as the bus pulled away, I saw a man with a duffle bag over his shoulder. It was him! We both ran to each other and, if it had been legal, would have dropped to the ground and done it in the road. We professed our undying love for each other and how much we had missed our kisses. I was beside myself with excitement but fear stayed close to me when I thought of him meeting Mama. The same fear I already had that one day he would leave me.

We walked the short distance to the apartment and I could see John's shock at how small it was.

"It'll be ok until I get a job," he said. "Where is your mother?"

I explained that she was with Big Boy and he would meet her soon enough. We had a lot of love making to catch up on and should get right to it, which we did.

The first time Mama saw John she said to him that he must be the *Yankee boy Carol had talked about so much.* He confessed that he was and told her it was a pleasure to meet her. I could tell she had tried to fix herself up a bit, wearing a cotton dress and sandals, but her hair had only been combed through quickly and I saw Big Boy sneaking' in the door behind her. I began to wonder if there was going to be enough room for the four of us to talk in such a small space, especially with Big Boy taking up most of the room. Introductions were made all around and Mama and Big Boy said they just stopped by to see John. I was happy about that and even more so when they left. Seeing Mama with another man after what had happened just three years ago was agonizing. Every time I saw Mama I wanted so badly to ask what had happened on that day in 1967, but I knew it could never happen. The doctor's warning would sound in my head; Mama might not be able to handle a conversation about Baby Cobb and it could destroy her mentally. I had to keep it to myself but constantly wonder, imagine, or conjure up images in my head over and over with never knowing why it happened. Did Mama think about it? Did she remember it? Had she ever talked about it, even with a doctor? With all my might I hoped we could someday discuss it, but instead, I was doomed to resolve it only in dreams. Grams would come to me in the night and tell me it was alright and I would wake up and remember her as if she had physically touched me. Sometimes I caught myself staring at Mama, wondering what was happening in her head, but I knew it was all locked in there forever. I was trying my best to handle it all without medications, proving Dr. Ward wrong. The walls I had built seemed sturdy, for now.

John got a construction job making decent money and we eventually moved into a bigger place, but not by much. It did have two bedrooms, one for Mama, and a separate living room and kitchen with one bath. It was on the prestigious Victory Drive and sat behind the main house, which was yellow brick with a big front porch. Big oaks filled the yard sharing their presence with a fig tree and a mimosa that curled its leaves when touched. Flowers sprung up in borders all around the big house and short, stubby little bushes squatted in front of the small house. Our little place had once been quarters for the help to the big house but when those days ended, it became rental property like many places in Savannah. Mama stopped seeing Big Boy or anyone else for the time being.

John and I were crazy for each other and spent our nights love making but still we had to work. We all took the bus to our jobs until 1972 when we were able to buy a vehicle. All of us smoked cigarettes but Mama was the only one who drank coffee night and day. True to southern tradition, John and I drank sweet tea that was more like syrup than tea.

Towards the end of '72, I got pregnant. I wasn't sure how I felt about it and started thinking about what a bad mother I had been when I left Sheila. Grace and James had brought her to see me once after we had moved to Victory Drive and The Beast kept asking if John and I were married. Being around her was something I hoped never to experience again, but this time it was for Sheila. She was cute as a button and looked exactly like me. John and I played with her until they left and it was obvious The Beast still had tight reigns on the family. I didn't know when I would see my daughter again. Once, when The Beast and I were alone, she said to me, "You know you'll never have Sheila." I had known that from the beginning and was too afraid of her not to believe her. I really thought she would hurt me.

It worried me how Mama would react to my pregnancy. I didn't know why it did except that it might bring up unpleasant memories for her that she may not be able to cope with. At the same time, I was afraid of my own thoughts. I did not want to have another baby that wasn't planned or when I wasn't married but I never thought about not having him. Him: I knew it was a boy right from the start and I was not wrong. As soon as I told Mama, she reached for a cigarette and headed for the coffee pot. I knew it was making her nervous. Did it trigger something, the thought of being around a newborn? I couldn't even ask. I should be walking on clouds instead of eggshells, I thought. The one thing I knew for sure was I would have someone to love and love me forever.

John was happy and all along I told him it would be a boy. There was no ultrasound or any way to know, it was just something I knew. We painted the room blue and I asked everyone for boy clothes while friends laughed at me. But, on July 9, 1973, Zachary Seth Hayes came into the world as much of a boy as anyone could ever be. I was thrilled, scared, but thrilled.

I had twilight sleep during the delivery and didn't remember anything. One of the nurses told me that I kept saying "Mama why did you do it?" as they were waking me up. Nonsense, I thought. When I woke up in my room, Mama was sitting in the corner smoking. Yes, everyone smoked everywhere in 1973, including in hospital rooms. I asked if she had seen the baby. As her leg bounced up and down, she told me no, that she was waiting until later. Soon the big door to my room opened and the nurse came in holding Zach, with John on her skirt tails, grinning from ear to ear. The nurse laid him in my lap and Mama held her position, not even getting up but puffing her cigarette nervously.

"Do you want to hold him, Mama?"

"No, not right now," she said quietly. I understood and didn't press again.

We took Zach home three days later in our new vehicle. Mama was still at the house with us and shared a room with Zach. I was ashamed that I worried about my own mother being in the room with my baby when I knew she never had been part of what happened. It was more about her hurting herself or looking in the crib and being reminded of the past. I was afraid of her being driven over the edge and it would be my fault. Worrying that Mama would hurt anyone never entered my mind. She had never hurt anybody in her life.

As Zach got older it was obvious Mama was becoming more comfortable around him. She wouldn't hold him until he was able to hold himself up so he went almost a year before his grandma would caress him. When he was in my arms, she would pat him on the back and began to call him Zackie. She was trying to be a grandma, but she just didn't have the means of showing her feelings.

We stayed in the little house for a couple of years and in 1974, I was walking down Victory Drive when across the street I saw a tall, thin girl with long brown hair. We noticed each other at almost the same time and lo and behold, it was Ricki! I was in disbelief. I had not seen or heard from her in several years and had no expectations of seeing her again. I had asked Mama but she didn't know what happened to Ricki. I ran across the street and we were both shocked, even more so when we found out we had been living across the street from each other for two months. We stood on the sidewalk, smoked our cigarettes, talked and asked each other all the usual questions that friends ask after intermissions in their relationship. I told Ricki that Mama was at the house, so we headed back there.

Through the screen door Mama saw us coming.

"Well, Lord have mercy if it isn't Ricki! How you been, Ricki?"

They had an instant bond to each other if only through tragedy. We sat in the house and talked about the last few years. Mama brought up the hospital with a single comment:

"Wasn't that ole hospital just a horrible place, Ricki?"

"Yes, ma'm."

Neither one of them wanted to go any further with that topic so we moved on to other things. During the afternoon Ricki played with Zach and after several hours John came home and met her. In her I had a friend who shared stories of strange and frightening events in the hospital but who did not know about why Mama or I had been in an institution. There was no reason for Ricki or anyone to ever know. Over the years I even saw therapists that I didn't tell. It was too painful and embarrassing to me. It hurt to imagine that someone could think of my Mama as sick. When most people met her, they thought nothing was wrong and I wanted it to stay that way. After all, if you can't see it, it doesn't exist. A lot of people thought of mental illness that way but the same people thought nothing of having faith in God. The only persons I had ever told were Dr. Ward and John, because I just had to.

We had all made friends through work, and also people who smoked weed had a tendency to run into each other. John and I had a friend whom we introduced to Ricki and in 1974 they were married. We were a friend quartet now and went to movies and events together, all the while enjoying each other's company and becoming good friends.

Mama was always on the move. She had a hard time being still and walked as much as ten miles a day, even in the middle of the Georgia summer. After one of these long walks one day, Mama came through the door beaming and going on about this wonderful man she met downtown in a park. He used to be a doctor, she told us, and owned a house out on the Isle of Hope, an older community on the Southside of Savannah near the water. A beautiful place that was picture perfect, with houses surrounded by live oaks covered in Spanish moss and big magnolia trees, exotic shrubs, and delicate flowers, with the intra-coastal waterway at the end of the two roads that led in and out. A mirror image of most of Savannah itself. This news was supposed to be exhilaratin' and excitin' for us just as it was for Mama. She couldn't stop talking about this man whose name was Ed and he would be by tomorra' to meet us. Oh, thrills, I thought to myself. Thank God her relationship with Big Boy didn't last long.

Well, there he was, Ed, with one "d." He stood six feet or more, average build, glasses, light brown hair with a hint of red in a military crew cut, and lots of freckles and moles on his lily-white skin. He wore a fedora made of straw which was not too fashionable for the day but his short sleeve button up shirt and plaid shorts with sandals were ok. He took his hat off when he entered the house, like a gentleman would do, and extended his hand. So far things were better than I expected. By then I had become Mama's parent partly due to her lack of common sense, which had always plagued her. As far back as I could remember, Mama had trouble with simple things like starting a car or getting out a broken light bulb. "Unplug it first!" I yelled. She had trouble understanding the intricacies of using a coffee pot so instant coffee was a godsend for Mama. I coached her on what to wear and how to do daily activities like wash dishes. Most times I would wait until she left the room and rewash the specks that remained on the ones she had just cleaned. I had to remind her to put her cigarettes out before she emptied the ashtray and not to leave the house when things were cooking on the stove. She almost caused a fire once when she left a pot boiling with eggs in it and the water boiled out, leaving the eggs to smoke up the house. As much as I tried, I could not tell her about men.

"Well, Carol, Carol, I've heard a lot about cha, about cha. Your mother here, here, has told me a lot, Carol, Carol, Carol, a lot." A lot about what? I was sure Mama would not and had not talked about *it*. How could she if she didn't remember anything, like the doctor said?

John and I tried not to laugh, not sure if it was a joke or if he really repeated everything. It was apparent pretty soon that it wasn't a joke. Every sentence had parts that were repeated so when I told Ed that I heard he had been a doctor, it took an hour for him to explain. It's also when his irrational thought processes became evident.

Ed explained that he had started Emory University but left when he realized they were trying to control his thoughts and you have to be careful about those things, those things, those, things. There it was. I asked Ed a few more questions about what he did for a living and such, but none of them brought direct answers so I was left confused with how he made a living. They both left to go to Ed's house after the stories and Mama said she would be spending the night. She was as giddy as a school girl.

Later Mama cleared up some things about Ed's life and told me he had come from a very wealthy family up around Macon. His mother had died many years ago and left Ed a trust fund, which was more than enough for him to live on. It was handled by a lawyer in Savannah and Ed would not get the lump sum of money until he turned fifty, which is quite old for that sort of thing but his mama must have known he couldn't take care of himself. Mama said Ed was kind and admitted he had some problems but they liked each other and got along well. Soon Mama was moving her things out to the Isle of Hope and moving in with Ed. We had been invited out a couple of times and the property was beautiful, with a ranch style white brick house that sat off the road and huge magnolia trees lining the front yard. There was also a fig tree and in years to come Mama would bring me fresh figs and large magnolias that would fragrance my entire house. There was an unattached garage in the back yard along with a carport. From the looks of it, the garage hadn't been used in a long time but had locked double doors. Surely I would never want to know what secrets might be hiding in there.

I thought Mama would be safe with Ed, and even though he seemed to be a little off the norm, he did seem capable of living a close to normal life. John and I finally had time to ourselves and with Zach, so life wasn't so bad. I had seen a therapist a couple of times but refused to take medication, neglecting the advice of the doctor. Nightmares filled my head almost every night and the same ones repeatedly. Sometimes they were about water and riding in elevators but the headless people were still there, three of them and white ghostly figures still hovered around me. I still dreamed of Grams, especially when I was troubled. She would just be there, in my dream, not doing or saying anything in particular, but I would feel her presence and remember it when I woke. Mama was still taking medication for maintenance but I became worried that she would forget or just stop when she moved to Ed's. I knew she shouldn't be without it and there was always a big concern of what could happen if she stopped. Would she tell Ed, I wondered, that she needed these drugs.

We got married when Zach was three and Ricki and Dale were with us. John had asked me what I thought about getting married like it was a business deal and I was ok with it now, since I had vowed not to get married because I was pregnant. It was a simple ceremony in front of a judge in South Carolina, held outside under a tree. No cake or celebration. Just a matter-of-fact ritual but I was so nervous and scared that I got sick before the ceremony. I knew I couldn't keep John and though he hadn't seen it yet, my wall was larger than he was.

John was making a little more money but enough for us to move into a larger house. We never had enough money to buy a house but we rented one just outside of town in a great neighborhood near good schools. I was pregnant again and going to have another boy, I was sure. The new house was situated on a corner lot with an attached carport with three bedrooms and a very large backyard. Zach was five when Adam Nicholas Hayes weighed in at 9 pounds, 10 ounces. As with Zach, Mama wasn't ready to hold him for several months. Being around children made her uncomfortable and I understood. We also had a beautiful little dog named Tammy who was the perfect companion to two boys. It was all perfect now. John, me, Zach, Adam and Tammy. Our neighborhood was full of kids and Zach had made a lot of friends, being five years older than Adam. Since we lived on the corner, our house was the Kool-Aid house, and all the kids congregated there.

Up until now, Mama was doing well with Ed and we would spend holidays together, sometimes with Ricki and Dale. They had a daughter a year younger than Zach and then another girl right after Adam was born. We were one big happy group. Dale and John even worked together sometimes and we were all very close. But not close enough for me to tell Ricki about Mama and 1967. I knew for sure that Mama had told Ricki nothing about her past, just as I had not.

Three more years went by quickly and Zach was in school and Adam and I stayed home every day while John worked. I still loved John in my heart but was having a difficult time with the physical part. The passion that comes with new love was easy for me, but when things settled down, I didn't know how to have a real relationship. I didn't want John to hug me, much less have sex on a regular basis. I could not commit to loving or trusting anyone and was not about to accept the concept that someone could love me. I had lived my life without being touched after Grams died and I liked it that way. Except for the affection I showed Zach and Adam, I didn't feel the need to let anyone else in my world and started to push John away. I had built my walls on a solid foundation and was more determined than ever that no one would get through, except for the boys. I knew I could love them and let them love me with no restrictions. Loving them was different and easy, unlike adult relationships of any kind. It was unconditional love, like Grams'.

Then one day when I was in the shower a vision of the baby wrapped in a green and white towel attached itself to my brain and wouldn't let go. It was all there again right in front of me. I was in an all-out panic, starting to think I should hurt myself, but I didn't want to. The feeling would not stop. Zach and Adam were both outside playing with the neighborhood kids and I couldn't let them see me. Quickly I got out of the shower, lit a cigarette and thought about knives. I couldn't bear to go to the kitchen. I didn't know what I would do if I picked up a knife so I made myself pick up the phone. The wall phone was just inside the kitchen but I knew it was the thing I had to do. Shaking uncontrollably, sobbing, I tried to dial the number. It was a rotary phone and it seemed to take forever. Three rings and I heard the soft voice on the other end of the line.

"Hello."

"Ricki, I need help! HELP ME! I think I'm going crazy!"

"Did somethin" happen? What's going on?"

"There's something I have to tell you. I've never told you before!"

I was breathless and almost screamin' into the phone. All along I had been troubled about telling Ricki or anyone about my past. I didn't think they would like me anymore or else tell everyone they knew. It always had to be a secret. Mama couldn't have told Ricki at the hospital. She either pretended it didn't happen or didn't remember that it did. I was never sure.

It began to pour out of me like water out of a bucket. My voice shaking and my body trembling all over, I told my best friend about finding a baby in the freezer, Mama's arrest, and the reason she met both of us in the hospital. All the while I was wondering what Ricki would think of me. I had left everything in my life behind. All my school friends, my daughter, and anyone who knew me back then. I was sure the town of Swainsboro would never forget me or Mama and seeing that place or the people was an unbearable thought. It always made me shake and feel sick just thinking about it.

"There's more," I told her as I started to shake a little less. I had calmed enough to sit down and continued talking on the phone. I think Ricki knew not to come over and maybe sensed that it would be too hard to share face to face. Sheila was the next story. Ricki listened without interrupting. She didn't ask questions like I expected, but listened like a friend. It took me about thirty minutes to get the story out, talking as fast as I could to purge myself of the demon directly. Afterwards, Ricki asked if I was going to be alright and told me that it would never affect our relationship and, of course, she would never talk about it if I didn't want to. I knew I had to see a therapist again, but still refused to take medicine. I was a victim of my own thoughts and just needed to control them better. I told myself that all the time and could be quite convincing.

I went to a new therapist and saw her every week. The first day there, I told her I thought I was crazy and she tried to convince me I wasn't. I told her stories of stress in my life with raising two boys and not really wanting to love my husband physically, but not a word of Baby Cobb or Mama. Not for weeks. Aside from seeing the therapist, I also had group therapy every week. I listened to their stories and they were about rape, parents that didn't love them, or anti-social behavior. This seemed to be the case in every group therapy session I attended over the years. I was terrified I would bring up my past and people would stare at me like I was weird, or worse, say they remembered the story. I felt I was better off to just keep it all to myself but mostly it was about not hurting Mama.

Chapter 16

*Mama and Ed*

John and I weren't getting along and it was because of me mostly. He had his bad habits, like not coming home after work and still buying pot to smoke, but that wasn't it. I just couldn't love him. Aware that I was pushing him away, it didn't stop me, mainly because I knew everyone left at some point so I might as well help move it along. It was easier to accept if it was my fault than it would be if he left me, but either way I would blame him.

Mama and Ed began having problems, and she started calling me to pick her up and bring her to our house until the riff quieted down. Ed was increasingly becoming more paranoid. He didn't want Mama to step outside the house not knowing who might be out there. He would let the phone ring without answering it so the machine would tell him who called. Sometimes I drove out there to see if things were alright when he wouldn't answer the phone for days. He and Mama would leave every day around eleven and "go to town for their one meal of the day at a restaurant in Savannah, usually a buffet. Ed had told Mama to stop cooking after she left the stove on several times and almost caused a fire. Ed would eat at the buffet for hours, from noon until two or three in the afternoon. He was asked to leave several places in town and told not to come back. We never knew how or why he ate like that; maybe it was his only meal so he thought it should be a lot. No matter where he ate, he would sit at the table for hours to eat. We all started out trying to be polite about it and sitting with him but soon realized he didn't really know or care that we were there or not. He would continue to talk like we were there and Mama said it was ok. "Um, um, um. Shore is good food, Jessie, Jessie, Jessie."

I really didn't mind too much at first since it was only for a day or two at most before Ed would call and say he was coming to get her. Their relationship was an oddity and hard to understand to an outsider. Neither of them could love or show affection.

Once I went to hug Ed and he stepped away mumbling something about being careful of catching, catching, catching things. They survived each other but the road was starting to buckle. Mama seemed to know that Ed wouldn't let her stay gone for long and even when she cussed him up and down on the first day, by the third she had mellowed and gone back to him. She was adept at pretending things never happened and that's exactly what she did. It was impossible to figure out what was going on in those heads. Their eyes were not a path but rather a road block.

When Mama was at our house during her riff with Ed, she just smoked and drank coffee when she wasn't walking. As far back as I could remember Mama walked a lot. These days she was walking five to ten miles in an afternoon. The more troubled she was the longer the walk. She loved Tammy, our dog, and the two of them walked five miles to mall whenever Mama was with us. Tammy would wait outside for Mama and they would walk home together. Lots of people knew Ms. Jessie and Tammy by name. People sometimes would offer to give them a ride, even the dog, but Mama replied they would just meander on down to the mall but thank you so kindly. Tammy waited for Mama to come out of the mall, too, which never took long.

Mama would try to make conversation with Zach and Adam but they were young and only cared about playing outside. She had started to babysit a few hours at a time for us since the boys could play on their own. I never stayed gone too long because I knew that Mama couldn't handle a crisis, like the sort little boys can create with ease.

When I first starting picking Mama up after one of her fights with Ed, she would be pacing back and forth in the front yard holding a paper bag with her belongings and of course, smoking. She would bring a change of clothes and underwear with just the essentials for a short visit. As time went on, it went from a paper bag to a small piece of luggage. The luggage started to grow and with the growth, it meant Mama would stay longer each time. Overnights turned into days and then weeks. No one liked her being there for those long periods of time, including me. I resented it and felt like she was interfering in my life, which was already in turmoil. I didn't want to be the mom to my mama. I wanted her to leave me alone. She had caused me enough strife as it was and she needed to grow up. I didn't want her around, I didn't want to be around John but I loved my boys and couldn't run away. Knowing my mind was breaking down again, I sought out a therapist but I still didn't see it necessary to tell them everything. I refused medications and insisted I was just going through a rough patch, like people do.

Years went by all pretty much the same with the situation between me, John, me, and Mama getting worse. Zach was thriving in fourth grade and Adam was in kindergarten. They both loved school and their teachers loved them. Every parent/teacher conference I heard nothing but praise and when they weren't in school they played outside with friends, staying so busy they were never any trouble at all. So often they were my salvation during those times when I thought I couldn't make it through another day.

When Mama was at the house, she would get up several times during the night to smoke and always made coffee when it got towards sunrise. She sat at the kitchen table with her cigarettes, ashtray, and cup of coffee. John would get up before daybreak for work, and as he entered the kitchen, Mama's quiet presence in the corner would scare the wits out of him.

"Jeez, Jessie, you scared the crap outta me!"

"Oh, I'm sorry John Boy. Let me fix you some coffee and somethin' to eat."

John would politely tell her over and over that he didn't drink coffee or have time for breakfast. It was mostly because he just wanted to get out of the house. He had two women there he didn't want to be with.

Mama was staying weeks at a time and it took Ed longer and longer to call and say he was coming to get her. She didn't seem to care. Mama was happy when she had her cigarettes and coffee and never asked for much else. Since she had no money, we bought Mama's cigarettes and coffee, which put another strain on us. John and I were pulling apart and going separate ways. I was still talking to Ricki but Dale and John had a falling out at work and didn't talk to each other. John started a business with a friend of his and I tried with everything in me to love my husband. At times it would work for a short while and I would let him hug me, all the while thinking how much I wanted to push him away. We were doomed but neither of us was willing to give it up, yet.

John was a terrific father and spent a lot of time with the boys. He took them fishing, canoeing, and some days let them go to work with him, just like the dog Tammy that he always let tag along. Since he was in construction and worked for himself, it was easy and the boys were allowed to swing hammers and use other tools, which made them feel grown-up and special. They loved John very much and I was glad for that since I couldn't love him the way a wife should.

By the early 80s, John and his business partner had gotten into financial trouble. They were without work and we struggled every day to put food on the table, but had done that many times before. Mama was off and on, more on, at the house and paying for her stuff on top of ours was stretching us both to the limit. She was staying months at a time. We started talking about moving to Illinois so John could be closer to his dad, sister, and brother. His mom and dad divorced when he was in high school and she had remarried and moved to Arizona. John's dad had driven down to see us a few times and helped us tremendously with our debts. I felt it would be fair for John to be around his relatives after all his time in the South with me. At least that's what I told myself. Truth was I wanted to get away from Mama and so did everyone else. I loved her and don't think the feelings of flight that I had were any different from any child being too long with a parent.

John and I talked to the boys and made our decision to move from Georgia. It would be hard for Mama but maybe it would force her and Ed to stop bickering so much. I broke the news to her the next time she came to stay and her reaction was, "Oh my Lord, Carol! That's so far away!"

I couldn't wait. John left to stay with his sister and get a job so things would be ready for us to move. Mama insisted that I shouldn't be by myself so stayed with me even more. The boys and I tried to include her in everything but she was driving us nuts with constant questions about why we were moving and how much it *shore was gonna be different with ya'll not here.* "Yes Mama, it will be different for us all."

Labor Day weekend of 1985, John's dad flew to Savannah to help us move. We rented a U-haul, and packed it to the gills. Mama and Ed were there to say goodbye and for an instant, I regretted the decision to move. Looking in Mama's eyes and seeing what might be a tear as she shook nervously made me think I was doing something wrong. Time would tell, I thought. We would all be happy once we got to Illinois and life would be wonderful once again!

Three days later we arrived in Illinois, so far north it was almost in Wisconsin. It was 32 degrees there and 95 when we had left Savannah. What had I done? Living in the South I had never seen more than an inch or two of snow. The first year in Illinois we had several blizzards and more snow that I expected or ever wanted to see. I always say that snow is beautiful as long as it's in a picture.

After crying for three months straight, I went back into therapy with no need to tell them anything about the past. The move was just too much for me I told them. That was all. Panic attacks started soon after that and Mama and I were on the phone every week, sometimes more. She said she was coping, but I wasn't convinced. The therapist wanted me to take medication and I refused, thinking I was strong enough without it with the words of Dr. Ward echoing in my ear: *You'll probably have to take them for the rest of your life.* NO I WON'T. Mama had to take them though, because without them she couldn't cope with everyday life.

This became evident in the spring of 1986 when, in the middle of the night, the phone rang. It was the Savannah police, telling me they had found Mama wandering on River Street and she didn't know her name. River Street is the oldest area of Savannah directly on the Savannah River lined with cobblestone streets. It's filled with gift shops and bars that close by two a.m. but Mama wouldn't visit a bar or have money to spend in a shop. They found one piece of paper in her cigarette case with a local phone number on it, and it was Ricki's. The police had called Ricki and taken Mama to her house and called me from there. They handed the phone to Ricki and she told me that Mama was in bad shape, shaking, and not answering questions, so she would put her to bed and take her to the hospital in the morning. I thanked the police department for being so kind to follow up with the phone number and paced and smoked waiting to hear from Ricki and the doctors. I wished I had some medication to help calm my nerves. The stress was unbearable. John was working in Virginia and the boys were sleeping but I had to wake them up in a few hours for school...if I made it until then. I had always had trouble with turning off my mind, it never stopped, and now it was spinning, conjuring up bad thoughts.

The phone rang. Ricki was there with the doctor and the news was not good. Mama had suffered a major setback. She didn't know her name or who Ricki was, and she was convinced that I was dead along with John, Adam, and Zach. When I told the doctor I would leave Illinois right away for Savannah, he told me to wait two weeks so they could get her medicated, and maybe it would help. He said Mama would not even know I was there, at this point.

What had I done? I had been the only constant in Mama's life since she had left the hospital. She was my daughter now, just as Sheila was and my child, just as Adam and Zach were my children. The only thing to bring me any peace was Ricki. She visited Mama every day and kept me updated. Mama was showing no signs of improvement and still insisted to Ricki and the doctors that we were all dead. I let this go for two weeks and had so much guilt that I found it hard to go on without seeing Mama for myself. I was sick to my stomach every day, going without sleep and smoking like a chimney.

Ricki picked me up at the airport in Savannah and we went straight to see Mama. The hospital was much nicer and cleaner than Central State in Milledgeville, with light colored walls and modern furniture. At least she wasn't in an asylum like before. The nurse asked us to sit in a waiting room, which was furnished with two couches, end tables, and a chair. Pictures hung on the wall but they were of bright big flowers and not old southern oil paintings that had dimmed with the years. Yes, quite a change.

I was nervous when they brought Mama out holding her by the arms. I reached for her as her glazed eyes stared directly though me. We sat on the couch, Ricki and I, on either side of Mama as I said "Mama, I'm here now." She continued to stare ahead looking at something only she could see or perhaps nothing, darkness. It was hard to tell. Slowly the words started to come.

"Carol's dead, John's dead, they're all dead."

"NO MAMA. I'm Carol and I'm here. John, Zach, and Adam are all at home. Everyone is ok. We just don't live here anymore."

She quietly repeated her words, indicating she didn't hear me or believe me.

"Mama, I'm touching you. Do you feel it? Ricki is here, too."

"Ricki's dead, Carol's dead, they're all dead."

There was simply no way to convince her. She was locked up again. I felt the only thing to do was to spend time with her and tell her over and over that it was me and I was alive. Ricki and I went twice a day and did just that, with not a hint of improvement. The doctor thought it would take weeks if not months and reminded me that I should not have come this soon.

He was arrogant and showed disrespect to Mama and me by thinking no one could save her but him. I told him so and he grinned at me, turned and walked away.

Day four came and once again on the same couch with Ricki and me on either side of Mama, I stroked her arm telling her over and over it was me, Carol. I was alive and so were John, Zach, and Adam. Her heard turned toward me.

"Carol, is that you? What are you doing here?"

The crisis was over and we explained what had happened but that she would get better now with the medication and treatment. The doctor thought she probably had stopped taking the meds and, with me leaving, the devastation was too much for her. Now I had to tell her in just two days that I had to go back home to Illinois. The time came and she said she understood. "I'll be alright." She promised not to go off her meds again and she went back home to Ed. He never came to visit her, mainly because he was afraid of hospitals, and mentioned earlier that he thought they might not let him go home. He was serious and had every right to be. A couple of years before Ed had become delusional and thought a school bus sitting in front of his house was someone trying to kill him. He shot up the inside of the house. Somehow, Mama talked him into stopping the shooting and convinced him to put down the gun while she called his lawyer. She knew the neighbors would call the police and Ed's lawyer handled everything for Ed including trying to keep his sanity in check. After the lawyer, she called me and I called Ricki. We rode out there, and Ed had been taken to the mental ward already. Mama was in a tizzy as were Ricki and I. They admitted him but he was out in three days and nothing ever came of it. He lawyer took care of everything and life went on as, well, normal. Ed was extremely paranoid and kept the window curtains closed day and night. He was a pack rat with newspapers and magazines piled on the dining room table in stacks three to four feet high. He and Mama thrived off each other most of the time but there was just no understanding any of it.

Back in Illinois John didn't seem too concerned about Mama and I couldn't blame him. We had continued to grow apart and as years went on we just stopped loving each other the way a man and wife should. We focused on the boys and John spent every weekend at the river, where his dad had a canoe business and did very well at renting them out on the weekends. Sometimes John would take Zach and Adam but even when he didn't he would spend the entire weekend without coming home. We barely spoke to each other and I liked it that way. I knew our entire lives together that he would leave someday and now it would be soon. I just wanted to get it over with.

I made arrangements to speak with Mama's doctor once a month to make sure she was on track with her meds. Mama and I talked every week and she assured me she was fine. She and Ed were not getting along again and Ed would call me and tell me things. "Carol, your Mama, well, well, well, she almost burned the house down" or "she left the refrigerator door open and all the food spoiled." I joined the local Mental Health Alliance and went to group sessions but again never talked about what happened in Georgia. Mama was sick and needed my help was all they needed to know. I talked to people there and found out I could get housing for Mama through the state of Illinois but not without a lot of time and paper work. I started the process first and then told Mama I wanted her to come up north, with me. She hesitated but agreed it would be good to get away from Ed. All the arrangements were made for Mama to stay about a half hour away from us in a group home. I worried when they said she would have to share cleaning and cooking one meal a night but it just had to work. We only had two bedrooms and the boys had to share.

Mama came up on the train with everything she owned in a large blue suitcase that Ed had bought for her years ago. When we talked on the phone I explained she would be living in a group home and have responsibilities like doing her laundry and cleaning. She said that was fine and she was ready to get away from Ed. He, on the other hand, did not like the idea one iota. He called me every day, telling me I should not be doing this to him;

taking Mama away. Reasoning with Ed was like trying to explain a grapefruit to an orange. I told him it was just going to happen because Mama wanted it and he needed to accept it.

"Oh Lord, Oh Lord, Oh Lord, Carol. Why would you want to do this, do this, do this to me and your Mama? What have you done?"

At times, I felt sorry for Ed, just like I felt sorry for Mama. Neither of them had anyone in their lives except each other and me. Until he met Mama, Ed had no one but a woman he knew from the town he grew up. He had a strained relationship with a sister but they never talked.

In September, Mama arrived and spent the first night with us on the couch. She was exhausted and looked frazzled after the two day train ride. All of us got our three pats on the back as expected. Her hair was grey so I told her I would color it for her before we went to her new home. She always liked it when I did things like that and it made me feel a kind of closeness to her that I wouldn't have any other way.

When the morning came, the boys went off to school after telling Mama goodbye. They were never close to her and I knew it was because she was afraid to be close to them or anybody. The little grocery store where we lived had the hair color. We colored her hair, went out for lunch, and then to her new group home. There was a lady who stayed full time during the week and a man who stayed on weekends. Both were very nice and I was sure Mama would like them. The weather was cooler than what she was used to but not bad in September that year.

"Well, this is your new home, Mama. Welcome to Illinois."

We drove up to the old, very large house that was filled with trees front and back. The leaves had not begun to fall and the house obviously needed a paint job. We entered through the long, narrow kitchen and were met by the house lady, who introduced herself and told Mama that she stayed during the week. I could tell she was shocked at Mama's southern drawl but

Mama quickly cracked a joke about being the only "cracker" in the house. Mama was good at breaking tension with a joke, even when she felt tension herself. That part of her is within me.

After taking a tour of the massive house with four bedrooms and seven patients, Mama was told it was a co-ed house like most group homes and she said, "Aw, I don't mind, ma'am." Mama was required to cook one meal a week at night. That was an immediate concern since Mama had trouble with tasks of any kind and had almost set things on fire before. I think my nervousness exceeded Mama's but I tried to hide it. I explained to Mama that we would see her every weekend and sometimes she would spend Saturday nights with us. Everything seemed in order: I helped her unpack, made sure she had cigarettes and could make coffee anytime. We bought a big jar of instant Nescafe.

I put my arms around her and felt my three pats on the back. I got in my car and cried most of the way home. Sometimes remembering Mama the way she was, the way she looked when she was married to J.W., was hard. When did she become my child, and was I being a good parent by taking her away from all she had ever known? Her walks to Sandfly (a small nearby community) every morning from the Isle of Hope, the friends she had made just by never meeting a stranger or being one. Everybody loved Mama and many people knew her from her daily walks and stops at the Piggly Wiggly. I told myself it was the best for all of us and that took some convincing on my part from time to time.

Ed started back calling right away.

"Carol, Carol, Carol how could you do this yor Mama and me? She shouldn't be up there in that cold weatha! What have you done?"

"Please Ed, don't call me anymore," I begged. "This is hard on all of us but Mama wanted it and it's done. LEAVE ME ALONE!"

Right away Mama tried walking in the neighborhood. I really didn't know that much about Rockford, since the city was about thirty minutes from where we lived. After visiting her several times and listening to the news, it was evident the part of town she lived in was not conducive to walking, day or night. I told her to be careful and only take short walks around the block. She didn't like that. When I brought her to our house in the small town of Pecatonica, she was free to walk as long as she wanted. It was the epitome of the safe, small town, and she would walk miles in a day and luckily always found her way home. Our dog Tammy had died at the age of thirteen before we moved, and we had gotten a solid black lab/shepherd mix that we named Trouble. He remembered Mama from when he was a puppy and loved to walk with her. Everyone around town knew him by name so Mama was safe with his ninety pounds beside her, no matter where she was.

Ed continued to call and after a month he told me he had been calling Mama and she wanted to come home. The October weather had turned cold and the snow hindered Mama's walks. When I asked Mama if what Ed said was true, she shook her head side to side and said "Naw, Carol, I'm alright." I didn't believe her and knew it was a matter of time.

We had Sunday dinners with Mama at the house and she enjoyed seeing John and the boys, but especially Trouble. She always had affection for animals and showed them the love she was unable to give to humans. My marriage to John was coming to an end but as far as Mama knew everything was fine.

In December the weather was brutal, especially for a southerner. She was at the house with us and during dinner she quietly said:

"Carol, I just don't think I can live here anymore. I want to go home."

"What's wrong, Mama?"

"It's too cold and I can't walk. Ed's gonna get me an airplane ticket home."

"Alright, Mama. That's fine."

We continued our meal and when I took her back to the group home I told her to just let me know when Ed got her ticket. In two weeks she was gone.

Zach graduated from high school in 1991 and made his lifelong dream come true by immediately leaving for the Marine Corps. With John working out of state, Adam and I were home alone most of the time. When John did come home, we stayed away from each other.

I was working two jobs in different towns and Adam played every sport he could in school. The places I worked were nice enough to let me off for any of his games since they were sometimes over an hour away. John continued to only come home occasionally but was there for graduation, and after he left I found his wedding ring in my jewelry box. I filed for divorce in the fall and had the papers delivered to him in Virginia. I couldn't love anyone, much less let someone love me. It was all I could hope for that my children would be different. I was happy when I was miserable with no one to blame for anything. I liked solitude and without work or the boys, I would have been a recluse. It just seemed easier when you didn't have to deal with people or life.

Not hearing from Sheila for years, I had no idea where she was or how she was but I couldn't go back. That part of my life was too painful and allowing myself to have feelings for her might break me in half. That was my logic, warped as it was.

Adam and I were in the kitchen alone. I told him we needed to talk. He had to have known that his dad and I were not happy, I thought.

"Adam, things change, and your dad and I have decided to get a divorce."

He put his arms around me with a desperate hug and cried.

"I don't want things to ever change," he sobbed.

It broke my heart and I wondered how long I had been so good at hurting people.

Chapter 17

*Losing and Finding*

The divorce was final and I didn't know or care if I would ever see John again, although I hoped he would keep his relationship with the boys. They had always been so close. I got an apartment and Adam had a good job while he was going to college so he and three of his schoolmates shared an apartment. We weren't too far away from each other.

Mama and Ed were shocked at the news of the divorce and wanted me to come home to Savannah. The only reason I didn't go was Adam. He had been in first grade when we moved to Illinois and it was all he knew, so he wanted to stay. Up until then, I had thought so much about going home, not realizing that Adam would want to stay in the cold. I was disappointed but understood so the decision was made for me. It was ok because I loved my boys like nothing else. Zach was in the military and I was glad he didn't have to be around it all.

Soon after the divorce I met a young man (I do mean young) and we became friends. Terry was about half my age but we shared a kindred spirit: he was an old soul and I was an old fool. We started going to movies and out to eat and became friends. After a few months it became more than that but I tried to end the relationship early on because of the age difference, but he was persistent. I told Mama about him, explaining our age difference.

"Well, Carol, if you were a man they'd be pattin' you on the back like a good ole boy. Good for you!"

Within a year we moved in together and I found myself loving him in every way. It was the first time in my life I allowed someone to love me and I loved back. Very early on, I told him my life story, the story I had only told John and Ricki until now. I wasn't sure why I opened up to him so quickly or freely but it felt good, cleansing in a way. I thought maybe he would run after hearing my story, but he stayed. I told him there would be times when I would push him away but he said as long as I let him back in it was alright. I was in the best relationship of my life and I wanted so badly to make it work.

At first it was hard for Adam and Zach to accept me seeing someone so much younger, but after they got to know him and his good heart, they appreciated him like family, the same way his family had accepted me. It was, and is, hard for anyone to understand an age difference like ours, but I thought about Grams and her marriage to Mr. Frank. It was more acceptable for the man to be the older one, but I was going to set a new precedence, damn it!

Within the first year or so, I took Terry to Savannah to meet Ricki, Mama and Ed. It was Easter and Ricki picked Mama up and brought her to the house. She had lost most of her front teeth, her hair was very grey, and what little she had left sprouted out of her head. She looked like a homeless person and I was embarrassed and shocked. I felt ashamed for feeling that way about my own mama but I saw the look on Terry's face and even Ricki knew I would be surprised. Mama warmed right up to Terry and him to her as she asked just where in Yankee-land he was from and what kind of last name he had? We all laughed as he explained it was Lithuanian and said he never realized he lived in Yankeeland!

"Well, son, if you live north of the Mason-Dixon Line you're a Yankee. Oh Lord, don't ever bring up Grant to Ed. He hates Grant!"

We were all laughing and Mama told stories of some of the crazy things Ed had done. Like when they took a month-long trip to Russia and she was terrified he was going to say something wrong and they would end up in Siberia. Or how he drove his old '55 Olds down the Savannah roads, swerving to miss any potholes and had been pulled over many times by the police thinking he was drunk. No, he was just dodging potholes.

"Oh yeah, Terry, did Carol tell you he repeats things three times? I'm telling you he's just a nut."

We laughed so hard and it was a great day. It was obvious Mama was taking her meds and that made me feel good. Later Terry got to experience the Ed we had all talked about as we drove around Savannah dodging pot holes in the old '55 Olds.

"You sure are a young man, young man, young man Terry. Well, well, well, Carol must be pretty frisky herself!"

The fun never stopped! I was home with Ricki, Mama, Ed, and Terry by my side and life was amazing.

That was the first trip of many for us as we went to Savannah every year. In 2000 I changed jobs and starting working for a large retail company as an executive. It was a good job but long hours and of course in retail you work all the holidays that everyone else has off. Terry had gotten a promotion at his job and was also making good money. Zach and Adam were doing great and my life seemed as if it were coming into some sort of normalcy. It was too much for me and I started having panic attacks again and fits of crying where I couldn't stop.

"You'll probably have to take them the rest of your life." I had pushed back those words a thousand times and now I was choking on them. Was Dr. Ward right all those years ago? Would my life have been different if I had listened to him?

He had been right all along. Trying most of my life to prove Dr. Ward wrong, it finally dawned on me that I needed help. My brain wasn't wired right and I wanted to be like other people: be able to love and be loved. I agreed to medication and it helped me tremendously. I was a fool for waiting.

My job was going very well and life was as good as it had ever been. I was happy. I still felt the guilt of leaving Sheila, moving Mama, and divorcing John, but I was dealing with it all now, except I still could not contact Sheila. She was too far in the past and I had buried her too deep in my mind. I was embarrassed and ashamed of the things I had done when I was fifteen and if I were to let her back in my life, there would be too much explaining to do. Friends I had made during my career wouldn't understand, and I wondered what they would think of me if they knew. I had too many secrets for such a long time that I couldn't start letting go of them now. It was too late. My life was spent lying on a cliff every minute and believing someone was waiting to kick me off the side where I would never stop falling. I was always feeling a storm coming.

The other thing I didn't deal with or want to was Baby Cobb. She was always in the back of my mind, trying to push her way to the surface, and it took everything I had to keep her buried. No one ever knew about her except John, Ricki, and Terry. I never told the boys, but Zach had met Sheila when they were very young and he had memories of that. Adam didn't know anything. They knew their grandmother was somehow different but didn't know why. For years I had left Swainsboro behind and would keep it that way as long as I could, forever if possible.

Time was flying and it would soon be Christmas in retail, which meant no time off. It was my first Christmas at my new job since my training the year before and I was responsible for it all. It was important to succeed, for the sake of my career. Zach was very happy and had married while living in California. They had a daughter—my grandchild—and named her Savannah. Perfect!

On October 14, 2001, I received a call from Ed that Mama had been hit by a car and was in the hospital. It was hard to get information from Ed due to his repeating of sentences and his paranoia. He always had to interject his opinions of why it happened and "who they were after" this time. I lost my patience.

"Ed, tell me what has happened to Mama. I need to know that first!"

He still rambled on for what seemed like an eternity before he got to the facts. My patience running thin, I screamed into the phone.

"ED!"

Mama had been taking her daily walk and was just across the street from home when the car hit her. Ed blamed it on the neighbor but we didn't believe that's what happened. It was actually the neighbor who called the police and went to tell Ed. He wasn't accustomed to answering the door so she had to scream at him from outside.

"You know that woman across the street; she backs that car, that car, that car out of that driveway without even lookin'. She hit your, your, your Mama, Carol."

 The police weren't sure what had happened or who had hit Mama, and she didn't recall anything other than getting bumped. The neighbor called the police and ambulance and had someone wait with Mama while she tried to get Ed. After finding out that much information, I called the hospital and she was just being admitted. The ER doctor promised to call me back after the exam. Why was I in Illinois? I needed to be home, in Savannah. The guilt hit me like a boulder. The waiting was like time standing still. I knew that she was conscious and the injuries didn't seem to be life threatening or too severe. That at least was some consolation. The doctor called me back and said they were admitting her to the hospital due to the chest X-ray. They had found two small tumors in her lung. I was devastated. All the years of smoking had caught up with her even with all the walking and exercise she had done her whole life. I called her room as soon as I was able. She knew it was me on the phone and she told me the news herself.

 "I've got cancer." She followed this with her usual, "But don't worry about me, I'll be alright."

She had been saying that to me since I was a child but she couldn't believe it every time. I knew that in my heart and I'm sure she did, too.

After the tumors were biopsied the next day, the doctor called me with the news. Yes, it was cancer. I called Zach, Adam, and

Ricki. Terry and I made plans to leave for Savannah the next day.

Mama was admitted to the hospital on October 16, 2001, and had multiple tests to see how much cancer had consumed her already. Terry and I rented a car and headed straight to the hospital and found out Mama was down the hall having some tests. Ricki was already there, waiting for us. The nurse told us we could wait outside the MRI room. Soon the doors opened and a gurney rolled out carrying Mama. She was covered in a white sheet that almost matched her complexion. She looked thin and frail and had aged at least ten years, all within just a few months since I last saw her. I kissed her on the cheek and felt the bones in her face and hands as I took them into mine. She said hello to Ricki and Terry and we all went to her room together. It was quiet with us just sittin' and staring ahead. After a while, Ricki had to go home, but Terry and I stayed to meet the doctors. Mama was having breathing treatments a few times a day and other meds but she wasn't in a lot of pain. With Terry in the room, she called me to the bedside and told me she did not want to be hooked up to "all that stuff." I couldn't believe she was telling me now. We had just found out and I was holding out hopes of her getting better, although my heart knew I was pretending again. My father, Edd Saxon, had died of lung cancer in 1995. I never saw him or went to visit but his family told me they had tried chemo and radiation. I did talk to him on the phone and knew that it caused great pain. He was on a morphine drip that didn't seem to help. I was on the phone with a cousin who was in my dad's room when he died. I didn't cry and I felt no guilt.

The doctor came in and explained that Mama had two tumors in her right lung. They needed to do surgery to determine the course of action.

"I know your mama," the doctor said. He saw my surprise.

"I live on the Isle of Hope and everyone knows Ms. Jessie. I think we've all offered her a ride at some time but she had to have her walk. As soon as I saw her, I knew it was Ms. Jessie." All the words came from him with such compassion and kindness that it took me aback for a minute.

"Ms. Jessie has a strong heart and is real healthy and would live for a long time if this cancer hadn't gotten her. I'm sorry."

He went on to say the prognosis was not good but they would do everything and they did. He was giving us time to go back to Illinois before the surgery and time for Mama to gain some weight. I had never seen her so thin.

Around 1984, Mama had given me paper work that she had requested from Harvard Medical School to donate her brain. I was shocked and asked why she thought of that, and her reply was that she just thought it might help somebody. "My brain, it's sick, and maybe they could find some reason." Reading the instructions for the process determined for me that it was something I would not be able to deal with. As soon as Mama died, the doctors would have to "harvest" her brain and make sure it was shipped to Harvard immediately. I told Mama I was sorry, but it was too much. She seemed disappointed but she knew then it was too much to ask of her daughter.

The surgery showed the cancer had spread to her esophagus. None of the news was good and Mama knew it, too. She never broke down or shed a tear that I saw. Her inability to feel emotions was now in her favor. She felt fear and maybe remorse but there was something else happening. She was handling it all with an inner peace I had not seen before. While I fell apart, she was gathering strength. Had God come to her, I wondered.

The staff at Memorial Hospital in Savannah could not have been more helpful or kind. I worked with them to get a nursing home for Mama before we had to go back home. Mama's favorite place to walk was the beach, Tybee Island. With help from the hospital I was able to get her in a nursing home there. A room would be available in a week so Terry and I drove to the beach to tour the facility. It was clean, and fully staffed with courteous people willing to answer any questions. The covered patio at the back of the building faced the ocean which was just over the dunes. Patients could sit there and smoke so I knew it would be Mama's favorite place and she would like it that they served coffee all day. Wrongly, I had assumed Mama would quit smoking in an effort to try and save herself but while I held out hope, she knew it was too late.

Terry and I went back to the hospital to tell Mama about the home on the beach. Mama was as happy as could be when she was at the beach. Ed stayed inside the motel, afraid of the sun, but Mama started walking at dawn and continued throughout the day until nightfall. She found some kind of peace there that only she could understand. Did her thoughts not wander there? Did the sun and crashing tides take away some bad memories, perhaps? Or maybe she knew that Ed was at a safe distance but she was comfortably untethered for hours at a time.

Mama had tubes and wires connected to her and looked like an alien in a scifi movie. Breathing treatments were twice a day but I wasn't sure what they were supposed to do. She had never complained about pain or being sick but had said she just didn't feel good sometimes. They brought food regularly but she ate barely anything. Her hands and frail body shook with a slight tremor and her eyes had looked at everything in the room, except me. She was already disconnecting from it all and I understood. We were both good at leaving situations without going anywhere.

Although Mama had just been diagnosed, the hospital staff helped me work out the plans for hospice and gave me all of the phone numbers, addresses, and pertinent information I would need when the time came. The time was coming and they were trying to let me know gently that there were things I needed to do. I sat in the hospital office signing papers and chitchatting congenially about how nice it would be for Mama to be at the beach she loved so much. Planning a vacation.

Feeling better that she was being well taken care of, Terry and I headed back to Illinois. A big concern for me was Ed taking her out of the hospital because he was lonely. My being her power of attorney prevented him from doing that. At least that was one worry I could let go of. Ed had been to the hospital once, very apprehensively. He was always afraid they might not let him out if he showed up on the wrong floor. "Terrible, terrible, terrible about your mother, Carol. Um, Um, Um." As much as I despised him at times, I saw genuine hurt in his eyes and on his face and I felt very sad for him.

Mama got transported to the nursing home on November 3 and had surgery on her right lung November 26. Before the surgery though, when I couldn't be there, Ricki picked Mama up from the nursing home and took her back to her house to have Thanksgiving with her family. Ricki was truly a Godsend and cared for Mama like a daughter would. Mama loved her as much as she ever loved anyone.

We went back down to Savannah for the surgery, which only brought the worst news. Her doctor informed me there was no hope since the cancer had spread to her esophagus. He gave us the medical terminology which meant nothing but he was searching for words of comfort while he spoke. He was a kind man and treated Mama like a friend. Mama stared straight ahead, trembling and muttered, "I'm going to die." Foreboding.

I tried so hard not to break down but it was too much and I sobbed at her bedside. I wanted desperately to hug her, have her hug me, so we could cry on each other's shoulder but I had to do it alone. Terry and Ricki tried to comfort me all the time and I felt the love, but I needed Mama now. I needed her to tell me things. Things I wouldn't have to keep inside anymore. Things she needed to let go of. Please cleanse us both now, Lord. But I knew it wouldn't happen and wondered with the end this close, would there be a minute where she would whisper in my ear. When she would wait for just the right moment when she knew no one could hear but just us, and God. Would she look at me and say she remembered or that she never did? My entire life I never doubted that Mama had nothing to do with the death of that child. I believe she may have been pregnant although I, along with many others, just didn't notice it. I believe the trauma of what happened, whatever it was, was too much but she had no choices in what that bastard did ,nor did she even know until that day in August. I felt so uncertain, ashamed that I was thinking about these things, about myself, instead of Mama's pain. Even though she didn't complain they put her on morphine, but it didn't dull her wit. Mama always had a sharp, stinging wit about her which I chalked up to the Irish DNA, since I have it, too. I am sure she did not get it from Grams!

After a couple of days, I was surprised to hear her joking with a male nurse like they were long-time friends. She wasn't eating so Terry would go out and get anything she wanted, milkshakes, barbecue, just anything to try to get her to eat something. One night she wanted some sweet tea so off Terry went to the grocery store so she would have some whenever she wanted it. A few minutes later he walked into the hospital room carrying a big plastic bottle of tea.

"Carol, what in the world *is* that?" Mama asked as she just stared at the plastic bottle Terry had brought in.

"It's sweet tea," Terry casually replied.

"I've never seen sweet tea in a *plastic* jug before! God Lord!" answered Mama.

Well, poor Terry. He had no idea that neither the Old South nor my mama would ever consider drinking tea from a plastic jug. She smiled at Terry and laughed and asked him to pour her a glass.

Mama was moved back to the nursing home. I was anxious, so afraid for her and me, but still she seemed inwardly peaceful. I received a phone call in the middle of the night to tell me Mama had fallen going to the bathroom. I panicked at first but the nurse told me that she was not hurt at all, they couldn't even find a scratch, but it was their policy to let the relative know about anything that happened. I'm sure the law had statutes about these things, but it still made me feel I had her in the right place.

She had not asked me for cigarettes but like a child wanting candy, she had the nursing home call me and ask if it was ok for her to smoke. Of course, I told them. I can't deny her the one thing that makes her calm. Ricki's church was at the beach, not far from Mama, and she would visit Mama every Sunday and take Mama out for ice cream. Every Sunday. I never asked her to but she was that good of a friend. Sometimes we would laugh when she would tell me how Mama would say, "That shore was good, Ricki! Let's have two!" Ice cream topped off with a cigarette and a cup of hot coffee. That was my mama. She also made sure Mama had cigarettes and bought her cartons at a time. It broke my heart that I couldn't be there but Ricki made sure Mama wanted for nothing. I could never have a better friend. Sometimes people would ask if we were sisters and we laughed and said yes.

I would call Mama a couple of times a week and most of the time they would laugh and say they would have to find her.

"Ms. Jessie is always on the go" they would say.

Usually we would say almost in unison to check the veranda and most times they could find her there in her wheelchair smoking her cigarettes. Other times she would just be wandering the halls or chatting with someone. Ms. Jessie never met a stranger and she raised me just the same.

Hospice came in not too long after her admittance to the nursing home and I met them on my next visit. They asked things like what Mama liked to do. Would she perhaps like someone to read to her? Would she like to listen to music and, if so, what kind? Her religious beliefs, and did she like to be massaged? Absolutely not. I explained that she was not comfortable being touched. I don't think she even liked having her hair done all that often because someone had to be touching her to color it. Once a week a hospice person drove the eighteen miles from Savannah to Tybee to sit for hours and read to Mama. The pastor from Hospice became friends with Mama very quickly and he was seeing her two or three times a week. I had left God out of my life for many years, feeling he had abandoned me at a young age. Now Mama needed him and I prayed it wasn't too late, so without telling him too much, I told the pastor that Mama and I needed God with us now. He prayed with me and told me that he and Mama prayed together every day he was there.

Ed had also started to visit and I could see the sadness in his posture when he saw Mama in the home. It was obvious he genuinely missed her and was as compassionate as he was capable of being. When Ed first found out about the pastor visiting Mama, he asked me if I knew about it.

"Of course," I said. "Why are you asking?"

"Well, well, well, then you know that he's, he's, he's a black man?"

"Yes Ed, I am aware of that and Mama likes him very much. I don't think that has any bearing on anything else."

Ed took it further by saying he just wasn't sure that "it looked right" to have a black man visiting Mama in the nursing home. Sometimes you just had to laugh at Ed and change the subject. It was just his old southern way. That was the way he was raised and he really didn't know any better.

During her stay at Tybee, they took Mama by ambulance to Savannah to see an oncologist three times, once each during January, February, and March. This was mostly to adjust her meds to her pain level. Mama was in pain now, but there was no grimace on her face or indication of what she was feeling.

Here I was, in Illinois, a two- or- three-hour flight away from Savannah. I was holding onto a thread praying nothing would happen without me being there. Getting the quickest flight would sometimes mean changing planes in Atlanta. There's a saying that goes "you can't get to heaven without changing planes in Atlanta," which I was starting to believe was the God's truth.

The guilt continued to consume me and I couldn't sleep. I started calling Mama from work. Retail is not the job to have during

Christmas when you have personal problems. I knew I had asked for time off during the busiest and most difficult time of the year and had to feel guilty about that, too. One of my peers said he was so exhausted he could hardly go on. I felt it was a stab at me since I had left for a week a couple of times, but I told myself he was trying to make it a general statement.

Thanksgiving went and Christmas came, with me working the entire time. It's probably when I felt the most remorse, knowing this would be Mama's last Christmas. In the beginning of January, I was making one of my usual calls to the nursing home to tell Mama that Terry and I would be down there in a couple of weeks. She told me she would rather me wait until Easter and be with her then.

"Mama, we can come both times."

"No, no, Carol. Easter is early this year and it costs too much for y'all to be running down here that much. I'm alright so just come for Easter."

"Are you sure, Mama? I really can come both times."

It wasn't right. It didn't feel right but I let her convince me to wait. I tried to make myself feel better by telling her I would call more often. I got updates from Ricki, the pastor, Ed, hospice and the nursing home, so I felt in touch. My conversations with Mama were usually short and she did not like being on the phone. Always trying to engage her in conversation, I would ask about any new friends, or the food, or tell her I knew how much she liked her ice cream every Sunday. Ed and I would call each other occasionally and Aunt Roxie and Uncle Austin were able to visit her at the home, as well. Aunt Roxie called to tell me she thought I had picked a good place and she was able to meet Pastor James and some hospice folks. She was trying to make me feel better but guilt doesn't let go with words.

Terry and I continued to work and I started really looking forward to our trip. Easter was early, March 30, and the time would fly with all the after-season work I had to do. Adam was going with us but Zach and his family, with a new baby girl, wouldn't be able to make it. I was ok with that and thought we could get together another time.

I booked our flights and we left on Thursday the 27th of March and planned to stay until Tuesday after Easter. It was warm in Savannah, which made our planned trip all the more inviting, and Mama living on the beach didn't hurt either. Seeing Mama and seeing the ocean would both be a treat.

The beginning of spring was finally on its way. I had many conversations with Mama, who was looking forward to us being there, especially being together on Easter Sunday. Ricki and I were always excited when we got to spend time together, it seemed so infrequent, but being like sisters we embraced the chance. I never felt the need to push Ricki away. Along with my children, she was in my safe zone where it was possible to be as close to me as my personal law allowed.

The day came when Terry, Adam, and I got on the plane for Savannah. We rented a car and went straight to Ricki's. Even at the end of March Savannah was very warm, and the cooling winds off the beach on Tybee were unusually warm. I couldn't wait to see Mama and we went as soon as we could. Terry, Adam, and I walked into her room and I put my arms around her. I could feel her bones through the thin sheet as she lay on the bed. Her hair was solid grey and her blue eyes had faded but still seemed to illuminate her face. I told her it was me and I was finally there. Mama looked up.

"Is that Adam?"

"Yes Mama, Adam's here."

"And is that Terry?"

"Yes, Mama, Terry is here too."

I explained that Zach and his family weren't able to come.

"That's alright" she said softly. "He's got his own family now and ya'll gonna be here for Easter!"

There was excitement in her voice and it made me feel good that I was making her happy in a small way. Pastor James and a lady from hospice were in her room and they asked to speak in the hallway. The pastor told me he had really enjoyed meeting Mama, with her sense of humor. He read to her from the Bible when he was there and they had talked privately about the past. Was he trying to tell me something? I didn't have the courage to ask so I looked deep into his eyes, trying to find the answer to a haunting question I had asked myself in dreams. One I wasn't sure I wanted the answer to but I desperately, undeniably had to know. Knowing it was the only way my mind could ever unravel from the knot that gripped so tight. It had obsessed me, consumed me, and made me fear everything. I was empty with only a coating, a shell that people saw. The inside of me was empty, no emotions, no love, no warmth, and I screamed in silence so that no one could hear for fear they would see my pain. It always had to be hidden. If someone found out, my walls would crumble and only dust would remain. Living on a cliff, hanging by a thread, every day of my life. I never blamed Mama for anything. At most I resented her, but like every child does her parent at times. Whatever happened in 1967 was not by Mama's hands. She was a victim of her own gullibility, thinking lust and love were the same. Looking into the pastor's eyes once more, I trembled, afraid I might see the truth, terrified that I wouldn't. I averted my eyes from his, heavy hearted when there was no answer, but also relieved in a bizarre way. I would have to save myself, if I could.

Ricki opened her home to us as she always did and the three of us stayed with her starting on the Thursday we arrived. We all went to Tybee early on Good Friday and Mama was getting weaker. We asked for a wheelchair so we could get outside in the sun and be near the ocean she loved so much. She asked me to take her to the bathroom in the main hallway. Terry immediately went to help her up and with fear in her eyes she looked at me desperately, pleadingly, and shaking her head back and forth. I understood. She was embarrassed and saying my name quietly as she pleaded. "Carol, please don't let him," she whispered. Her voice was so weak and so soft that unless you were leaning close to her as I was, it would have been impossible to hear her. Terry muttered that he didn't think I would be able to lift her by myself but there was no question about it.

"I've got you Mama," I said, and reached to pick her up from the chair. She was nothing much but skin and bones and the dead weight was demanding but not impossible. I had to sit her on the toilet seat and take her off again and back to the chair. She had become too weak to help herself. It was obvious she had stopped eating, just as the nursing home had informed me when we got there. I tried to coax her to eat but she pushed food away. She was too weak and tired for company so we left for the day knowing we would have a full day together tomorrow.

Saturday morning we all went back to visit Mama. It was a gorgeous day, a true Tybee Island day, the sun bulging with balminess, a warm sea breeze, seagulls buzzing the dunes, and the smell of spring in every breath. A day that seemed like the Good Lord had commanded a performance just for Mama. I had to get Mama outside where she could enjoy this glorious day. She was too weak to go on her own so I requested a gurney and with help from the good people at the nursing home we made it to the shade tree just outside the doors, facing the beach. We surrounded Mama, Ricki, Terry, Adam and me. We talked to her but she was barely hanging on. Ricki's three daughters came to say goodbye. They had all grown up knowing Mama and spent holidays and birthdays with her. Ed and Mama had some good neighbors on Isle of Hope and some of them stopped by, too. They mentioned that they thought it was special that Ms. Jessie was at the beach knowing how much she loved it. I wiped sweat from Mama's brow while she made a tiny, quiet sound. I thought she was asking me to go inside so we did. Even under the shade of the big oak it had become quite warm for all of us.

Mama was getting weaker by the hour and I knew I had to spend every minute with her. It was getting late in the day and I told everyone to head back to Ricki's. Mama's room had a recliner so I would be comfortable spending the night there. "I'll see y'all in the morning." Ricki sang in the choir at her church which was just down the street from the nursing home so it worked out well that she could drop off Terry and Adam.

The night came and although Mama didn't register any blood pressure, she was breathing. I didn't understand any of this, especially how she could be alive, but the nurses assured me she wasn't in any pain. They told me her pulse was so low it wouldn't register so it was just a matter of time. I couldn't take my eyes from her face. She looked peaceful but was she? I needed to know that she wasn't in pain. The morphine would take care of that, the nurses said.

I lay down in the bed with her and put my face as close as I could to hers, feeling the very slight breath coming from her mouth, like a very quiet whisper. I talked to her, told her how much I had always loved her and that the boys loved her, too. Talked about the week and how good it was to be with her and how nice everyone at the nursing home treated all of us. I told her that being out in the sun yesterday was something I knew she would like, and did she smell the ocean and the salt air that she loved so much? "Did you hear the sea gulls, Mama? The sky was so blue, just like a perfect day at the beach." The room was quiet except for the slight ocean breeze coming through the open window blowing the sheer curtains slowly in and out. "I love you Mama." With barely any breath at all she managed to say *I love you*.

I went back to the reclining chair that sat so close to her bed they touched. The nurses came in all through the night, saying they were checking on us. They said it was just a matter of time and she would soon let go, when she was ready. The chair was facing Mama, so I was laying the opposite direction of her so I could look at her face, as I did most of the night. Sometime in the black of the night, before any hints of the sun rising, I went back to her bed. Lying down beside her again, I could still feel the tiny breaths, making me think she was holding on. With my arm across her frail body and my mouth up close to her ear, I whispered "Mama, you can go now. Everything is alright and I have loved you all my life. Goodbye Mama." I gave her a big hug and held onto her for a few more minutes, tears streaming down my face.

I went back to the chair, hoping I had said and done the right thing. I knew she was in a lot of pain now that couldn't be controlled with meds. She was suffering and I didn't want her to linger longer than she had to.

Being so exhausted I finally feel into a light sleep, afraid myself to let go, needing to be there with her. She called my name so softly I wasn't sure if I dreamt it. I went to her as she took her last breath and was gone. Her bedside window had been open all night and the gentle breeze continued like nothing had changed. The sun was just coming up over the ocean. It was sunrise, Easter morning sunrise, and Mama had left me. I lay next to her for a minute and knew she had been waiting to hear the words I had spoken to her during the night. "Carol, why don't you wait and come for Easter?" she had said to me, and now I understood why.

Slowly I made it into the hallway to get a nurse. Several of them came into the room and hugged me. They told me, "Your mama had planned this for a long time. She kept telling us you would be here on Easter Sunday. She had been talking about it since Christmas saying you would be back for Easter Sunday. Um hum, she shore did plan this." The nurses brought washcloths and a pan of water. They ran the cloth over her face and hands and then brushed her white hair while I sat watching. It was heartwarming how they cared for her. They placed her arms under the covers and straightened the bed until the sheets were crisply situated around her without the hint of a wrinkle.

I went to the nurse's station and called Ricki's house. I really didn't need to say anything. It was so early in the morning she knew what had happened. Easter morning and Ricki was to sing in her church choir for the service. She told me she would get Terry and Adam up and they would be there soon. The nurses had called the pastor and I didn't even know. He was there very soon and we talked for a while. He told me Mama had confessed her sins and God would take care of her now. Confessed her sins? The next thing the pastor said to me was that he would not be able to share any of the talks he and Mama had, except that she was a lovely woman whom he liked very much. My head was spinning, I felt sick, warm, cold, and confused. I told myself to just let it go now, let it go.

Terry and Adam walked into the room as I was sitting, looking at Mama's face, her mouth and eyes open, the life gone from every being. They both came to put their arms around me and we all cried. I asked Terry to leave me and Adam alone. As Adam sat in the chair at the end of Mama's bed, I fell to my knees sobbing with my head in his lap. "You never knew her the way I wanted you to, you and Zach. See how these people loved her? Everyone loved her. I want you to listen to what people say!" We cried together for a few minutes and he knew what I meant. I wasn't trying to leave Terry out but he had known Mama for only a short time and he knew the Ms. Jessie that everyone did. Adam didn't know her much, as an adult, so I wanted to create another, different, memory.

Ricki came soon before and after she sang for Easter service. I knew how much that service meant to her and on that day I thought it probably meant even more. I was so grateful she was able to do it.

Aunt Roxie and Uncle Austin had been waiting for my call. They had been able to visit Mama once and knew she wasn't doing well. We had kept in touch about every two weeks and they had been a big support system for me.

I had more phone calls to make and now I needed to think about the funeral service. In the South, funerals are held in three days. Always. The only exception would be to wait for a family member that was maybe in another country, but other than that, three days. The funeral director thought I was from the north, so he politely informed me that in the South, it's three days. I told him I was aware of that, being from the South.

I called Ed and felt so bad for him. As much as he drove me crazy, he and Mama had been together for almost thirty years and now he would be alone. The house that belonged to him was where the two of them lived for all their years together. I was grateful to Ed that years earlier he had planned both of their funerals and prepaid for everything. They would be together in a mausoleum, the highest crypts in the building. This was because Savannah often flooded, being below sea level in a lot of places, and Ed (being a little off kilter) was worried they might get wet. He and Mama's tombs were next to each other. "Do you want a crypt there too, Carol, Carol, Carol? Lord have mercy, ya know, ya know, ya know, Savannah floods all the time, Carol. We need to be up high so we don't get washed away!" I declined his offer but thought it was a nice gesture.

Understandably, some of the next few days remain a little blurry. I don't remember how soon I saw Ed but I do remember the first thing he said.

"Lord, Carol, I'm really gonna miss your mother, your mother, your mother."  He was pitiful and my heart genuinely ached for him. All the times I had shunned him lingered over me now and with everything else I had done, I didn't know if I could ever be forgiven. What was my destiny now?

I wanted to comfort Ed with a hug but he and Mama were the same and neither liked to be touched. Trying to make eye contact, which neither of them could do either, I said to Ed that I knew how much he was hurting. He shuffled his feet as if he heard it but had to move on. "Go on to the funeral home, Carol, Carol, Carol, and make all the plans. It's all paid for. Just do it the way you want, you want, you want." He didn't want to be a part of any of it and I was sure he wouldn't be able to handle even the least little thing. How was he going to survive without Mama, I wondered.

I was so grateful to have Terry, Adam and Ricki with me and felt I had the people I needed at the time. Terry went everywhere with me and helped me so much with the planning and the little things we had to do at the funeral home. Ed stayed out of it completely; until he found out I was using the "black" pastor to officiate Mama's funeral. He "just couldn't believe" I would have that man there in front of everyone. The funny thing is that Ed had a friend (using that word very loosely) named Sammy who was black and worked on Ed's cars. Sammy would also bring vegetables from his garden for them and Mama always talked about Sammy. She really liked him a lot. Just like she came to know and like the "black" pastor. Mama had already asked me to have her new friend officiate the funeral and I thought the way he had treated her and had been so kind, there was really no one else.

The days were long and hard and I couldn't get through them without breaking down several times a day. I cried myself to sleep and saw the pain in Adam, Terry and Ricki's eyes. I think the worst thing that could happen in anyone's life would be to lose a child but losing a parent is close. Especially when your relationship with that parent had been so atypical. Mama was never able to tell me she loved me, except for that hot summer rainy night in Georgia when she took me to the little store. I was three years old. The next time I heard her say she loved me was when she knew she was dying and I could tell it was not easy even then. I came to realize over my lifetime that we show love the only way we know how. Some are able to hug, kiss, wrap arms around each other and hold tight while whispering those three little words. For others, it's not so simple so we do it in other ways. My Mama's way was to buy me things, take me out for dinner, and give me money to go to movies. That was her way of showing me love. I just didn't know it until adulthood. I saw people hugging—my cousins, Aunt and Uncle—and it just made me think they were different. It was why I had Grams' love until I was fifteen.

The day of the funeral came and it was just the weather Mama loved. Sunshine and very warm, a true good Savannah day. Aunt Roxie, Uncle Austin, and my cousins, Cid, Suzanne, Lisa and Melanie all came from South Carolina for the funeral. I was thankful to have them there, as well. There were other relatives who came but I had not seen them in years and didn't recognize them until they told me who they were.

We got to the funeral home and I remember walking into the room to see Mama for the last time. I looked at her face and cried, wanting to hold her one more time. I laid my head down on her chest and tried to step away. I knew that people around me were crying too but I couldn't help them. I felt weak, as if I would faint, and then I heard the pastor start to speak. He talked about how he met Ms. Jessie and how they would sit and talk day after day. He said she was a lovely woman and had given her heart to the Lord. He said beautiful things and my family was very impressed with him and the service. We left for the cemetery and Ed had gotten us two limos so the family could all be together. It didn't take long to get to the mausoleum and there were chairs set up inside for everyone. This is really where I can't recall much anymore. I knew she was in the vault now and she was gone. I don't know what happened to Ed. I knew he was there but I couldn't comfort him.

We sat in the mausoleum quietly and did what people do. Reflected on a life that wasn't so perfect. A life of hard knocks and not much emotional glue. Years of mystery, rough seas with swells that only grew larger with time and would never come to a calm. Miss Jessie. Indeed.

Epilogue

The Georgia State Lunatic, Idiot and Epileptic, Asylum later became known as Central State Hospital and was Mama's home for three long years. At one time, there were 112 patients to one doctor. Treatments consisted mostly of electroshock therapy and strong anti-psychotic drugs to keep the patients calm. Today there are 25,000 unmarked graves at three cemeteries reminding us of the inhumanity suffered by too many. My stay at Talmadge Memorial was a much different environment. I saw Dr. Ward as much as three times a week and was closely monitored to make sure I was taking the right drugs for my condition.

Today a stigma still exists around mental illness but there are more options for treatment. Private practice facilities sprung up everywhere starting in the late sixties and now confinement in a hospital ward is usually short term. For me it took decades of mental hell before I realized there really is a chemical imbalance in the brain that causes me to be off kilter. It's no different than a diabetic needing insulin. "You'll need to take medication the rest of your life." If only I had listened, my life might have been more tolerable and less of a rollercoaster ride. I take anti-depressants and sometimes anxiety meds and like most patients, sometimes I convince myself I don't need them but in a few months I know better. I have a doctor who keeps me on track with my meds but I only see a psychiatrist a few times a year. I've talked it all through over the years and now just try to maintain my balance.

Some of my questions about what happened in 1967 were answered in the newspaper article I finally saw after forty years. I'll never know the real story but God has intended it that way. Did Mama tell the pastor anything she didn't tell me? I never had the courage to ask him. Some things are better left alone. I will always wonder what happened but in my heart, I know Mama was not a part of any crime, but instead a victim of a monster of a man. Having a baby was not a crime.

Ricki and I have been friends since 1968 and are as close as sisters could ever be. We talk almost weekly, visit each other every year, and rely on each other for peace of mind at times. Other than John and Terry, she was the only person I ever talked to about my life until I wrote this book.

Four years ago I got a phone call from Sheila. "Mama, this is your daughter!" I hung up on her. The past was coming back and it terrified me. A few days later I called her and we talked and cried for two hours, each of us trying to explain our feelings. A few months later I flew to Georgia with Terry and met Sheila and my grandchildren at Ricki's. We spend time together when we can knowing we'll never get back those lost years but grateful for the time we do have.

Terry and I have been together now for twenty years and they have undoubtedly been the best years of my life. He is the kindest, and thankfully for me, the most patient and forgiving man I could have ever hoped for. I still have crazy days, with depression and anxiety, but he has learned to cope with me like I've learned to cope with my illness.

Zach lives in the northwest and is an officer in the military, happily married with my beautiful granddaughter he named after the city I love so much.....Savannah. Adam lives in the Midwest and has a son and a daughter. All of my grandchildren call me Nana. In the beginning I had thought about them calling me Grams, but there was only one Grams to me and it will always be that way.

God didn't forsake me. He is with me every moment of every day and has blessed me beyond my dreams.


THE END

Made in the USA
Las Vegas, NV
20 March 2023

69394787R00100